DISTANCE LEARNING SUCCESSFUL FACTORS

JOHN LOK

Contents

Preface

Nowadays internet is popular to be used by consumers. Internet can be applied to different aspects, such as online commerce, online search information, reading newspapers, ebooks, listening music, even artificial intelligent technological mobile etc.

This book aims to explain how to apply online education methods to raise education quality and explain why online education method can solve graduated student shortage challenge more than traditional classroom education method. I shall indicate how online education method can raise educational quality and student individual learning abilities and education performance to online teachers between online education institutions and online teacher to achieve the raising graduated student number of productivity aim. Also, I shall indicate why online education methods can raise human education knowledge capital to affect long term graduated student number growth of education productivities and education quality raising.

It concerns whether how future online educational development trends. I shall indicate how online education can be applied to let students to know these knowledge, such as how to predict environmental pollution to reduce water or air pollution occurrence to influence weather poor change and earth warm natural disaster occurrence to influence human life.

I suppose online education will be one popular new technological education method to assist primary, secondary and university online teachers to teach their students from online classroom conveniently in the future. In this book, I shall give reasons and actual data and economist's theory to explain why online education can raise graduated student number more than traditional classroom educaion.

In the future, online education will be one new technological popular education tool to assist any primary, secondary and university teachers to teach their students from internet channel.

I shall indicate some developing countries in Asia, e.g. Philippines, Korea, China etc. countries. To explain why they ought follow US, UK developed countries to apply online education method to assist online teachers to teach their students popularly if they expect their graduated student number can have enough supplying number to their countries' employment market in order to solve human resource shortage challenge for any industy.

For this topic, I shall suppose online education method can raise online (teachers) human capital whose educational abilities and skills to be assisted to educate their online primary and secondary and tertiary schools students to shorten time to study to achieve graduate more easily to compare traditional classroom education method. So, future education learning method trend, online education method will be demanded to be increased, due to students feel it is convenient to learn at their home in the future.

In chapter one, I shall give reasons to explain why education quality and education productivity and online education method have close relationship. I shall indicate what are developed countries and developing countries whose traditional classroom education method's weaknesses and online education method's strengths. Then, I shall bring the cause and effect relationship to explain why excellent online education method can raise student individual learning abilities more easily.

In chapter two, I shall explain the reasons why internet channels through online teacher human capital teaching method can affect students who can reduce studying period to graduate fastly. I shall indicate student learning evidences to compare the weaknesses of classroom learning and the strengths of online learning in order to judge whether online teaching method can affect students can reduce studying period to graduate fastly.

In chapter three, I shall give evidences to explain why the growth rate of online graduated student number is more than the growth rate of traditional classroom learning graduated student number. In the end, my readers can attempt to make yourself judgement whether online education can assist students to learn more easily to compare to traditional classroom learning method in order to achieve easier graduation.

Prologue

Table of contents

Chapter 1

ONE

ONLINE EDUCATION HOW INFLUENCES ONLINE TEACHER TEACHING ABILITIES

Why do schools prefer to apply computer tools to teach teachers in classroom learning environment? Will internet tools replace traditional classroom to teach students to learn at their home popularly? Does internet tools can replace school computer equipments to teach students more easily and it can let students feel more easily to learn when they turn on their computer to apply online learning tools at their homes.

In schools today, nearly all classrooms have access to a computer. However, many schools mistake this as incorporating information technology into the curriculum. School staff need to research what IT is available and what would best serve the school's purpose, not simply purchase the latest equipment. There should be a policy stating how IT is going to assist pupil's development and what teachers want pupils to achieve. Staff members need to be clear about what they want IT to do for them before who can start incorporating in into their lessons. Hence, online education will be popular teaching method, due to classroom had been accepted to install computer to let students to use to learn. If every student can learn how to apply internet to learn, then who won't need to go to school, who can apply internet to learn at themselves homes. So, installing computers teach students in classroom will encounter more challanges more than teaching every students how to apply internet tools to learn at their home.

So, the only way information technology is going to be useful to schools is if all staff members are well-informed and fully supported absolutely. It is the principal's responsibility and should be part of the school's plan to ensure that all staff are consulted about the changes and that the change is carefully organized. It seems that any universities need to spend time to prepare how to change to adopt this IT and internet new technological educational method from traditional lecturer face-to-face oral teaching method if which expect future student emotion and teaching challenges will be solve successfully. For example, some teachers may be especially learnt if who have not had much experience with computers by computer professionals teaching , so computer training teachers are essential in implementing IT into the school curriculum. Staff members must feel involved in the process of acquiring technology and in learning how to operate it, in order for them to increase their confidence in using IT as a curriculum tool.

So, primary and secondary teachers , even university tutors are only going to be able to incorporate IT into their lessons if they are potential users themselves. Consequently, to achieve online education strategy success, schools need to train teachers how to apply school computer internet tool to teach their students to let they feel comfortable when theis students are apply internet to learn between their online teaching and online learning channel at their home more than installing computers in school classroom methods to teach their students.

In addition, teachers need to be aware that IT
within the classroom is extremely flexible, but that they need to

plan what purpose IT serves in eaach lesson. The skills of a student learning are the important part of any lesson, and it is the same with technology. It needs to be used and understood in all subjects in the same way as the ability to read is necessary for all subjects and must be used across the curriculum in the same way that pen and pencil are used in most subject areas in any primary schools, secondary schools, even universities.

Anyway, the best way to plan the use of IT in the classroom will be approached it as simply a learning tool that is more advanced and more existing and exciting than the traditional pen and paper in any primary and secondary schools and universities in the future. The most important reason, IT educational method will attract many students to choose the school to study. Because internet had reached the mature stage and it will be one popular teaching acceptance tool to any students. Thus, it is vitually important for students to be taught the strategies for using IT to let students aware that the contexts in which their traditonal pen and pencil learning and writing method will be changed to be internet and IT typing and learning method as well as teachers need to know what the appropriate use of IT is and what is not when it is important that students learn to use IT effectively. However, school IT education method is not better than student home online learning method. The reasons include as below:

First reason, for US online education development example, science and engineering subject students are more difficult to learn in school classrooms than students apply internets to learn at themselves homes. Nowadays, US played a critical role in establishing leadership in science and engineering (S&E) education aspect, however, the next generation of scientists will need to solve these science and engineering subject educational challenge.

For example, how to ensure future generations continue to reap the benefits of fundamental S&E research. They need to give big ideas of what benefits can be given to the next generation students. Such as US country science and engineering research will lose serious and non-value if it doesn't ensure what benefits can be given to the next generation. So, online educational method can be attempted to solve this science and engineering subject educatonal challenge, due to this subject students need to often to do research and experiment to prepare to finish their assignments. Internet will be one useful tool to help students to gather any science and engineering datas to finish their assignment easily. So, computers and internet must need to be used by students in student homes more than school classrooms. Students can apply internets to research science or engineering information to learn how to do any experiments, if they have any experiment difficulty, they can send email to ask teachers to let them to solve their enquires from internet channel. So, online learning is more flexible time arrangement to any students to learn more than school classroom fixed time experiment for science or engineering subject students.

The second reason, teacher (Human capital) has ability and efficiency of online education labor to transform computer (internet) technological raw materials and online teacher human resource capital into education products and services to raise education productivity growth and education quality raising.
The accumulation of online education human capital improves online teacher labor productivity and increases the more learning effectiveness returns and raising online education quality. However, a well educated background is essential to raise online education technology to develop online education productivity and education quality growth in Asia developing countries especially, instead of US, UK developed countries, due to Asia countries have many students, but the number of schools are very less to be supplied to Asia to study. Hence, online (internet) educational methods will be popular to be increased demand to Asia students.
In macro and micro economic view, the well online educated labor (human capital) is often as one of the critical factors to influence rapid education productivities and educational quality growth to the Asia developing countries' any regions or cities. Because any of these Asia developing countries, such as China, Korea, Philippines etc. countries which need have well online educated and

knowledgeable teacher labors to raise any schools' educational productivities and educational qualities growth. So online educational qualities and productivity and internet education tool both factors which ought have close relationship to cause the good or bad future student learning effectiveness and education or learning qualities raising in these any one of Asia developing countries.

The third reason, for the big population of student growth number example, China's student growth rate is larger than school growth rate. If China expect every students have enough chance to study in schools, but school classroom numbers are not enough to supply to students to learn. How to solve classroom number shortage challenge. I believe that online education is only one kind of learning choice method to let many China students have chance to enter school to learn. They do not need often attend school classrooms, they can apply internet to learn at themselve homes. I supposes China one school has 50 classroom and every classroom can let 30 students to attend in the school classroom. So, the school can let the maximum 1,500 students to attend all 50 classrooms to learn. However, if there are more 1,500 students choose the school to learn. The school can choose online education method, it means that every student can choose to learn at home from internet channel. So, the online learning choice students do not need attend classrooms to learn. Consequently, the school can let more than 1,500 students to study, due to some students choose to apply internet to learn.

However, China encountered online skillful teachers shortage challenge. Nowadays, China was an major industrial and farming country between 1960 year and 2000 year. However, after 2000 year, it began to achieve any commercial investment to raise GDP income and to raise more service provision nature of employment chance to domestic labors. e.g. financial investment, shares trading, hotels and tourism and airlines and restaurants and cinemas etc. service nature businesses commercial investment.

Moreover, the foreign investors were also attracted to set up factories to manufacture their products in China's country any area locations. It was possible that this foreign investors felt China's workers' wages were more cheaper than themselves domestic worker wages. For example, USA has the minimum wage legislation to protect it's domestic individual worker wage level.

Otherwise, China's individual worker wage level is compared to be paid more lower level to compare to USA's minimual legislative individual worker wage level nowadays. It seems China, Korea, Philippines etc. Asia developing countries need have well online educated teacher labors to help them to teach student to let students to learn easily at home conveniently. Because the developed countries' foreign well online educated labors, e.g. USA, UK etc. who feel whose countries can give the best salary compensation level and benefits to let them to support to work and to live in whose countries.

Why can the developing countries solve online skillful teacher shortage challenge? Due to China teacher salary level is lower than foreign developed countries' teacher salary. So the developed countries' well online educated labors won't choose to go to China to work easily. It seems those developing Asia countries which governments need to invest in online education sector to increase many knowledgeable online teacher human labors capital to assist them to raise whose online education technological productivity or online education service qualities and learning effective productivity. If any one of these Asia developing Asia countries still want to keep the competitive position in global environment in the future. So, these Asia developing countries, such as China, Korea, Japan etc. must need have good online technological education tool to train any aspects of high knowledgeable online education labors to be supplied to themselves society to satisfy their student learning demand in essential.

1.0 Online education is similar to online TV entertainment and online logistic communication and mobile communication development

● Online TV development

Online television channels, platforms, devices experiences and choice will be positioning entertainment consumer market for the foreseeabl future. The reason is onlin ebook, music entertainment has been popular. Why does online television won't be popular? Bloomberg business week website (2013) indicated that the evaluation of control technological development of portability technological tool: from 1975 year , the astraltune product had been populaar. The, 1979 year, Sony walkman had reached the 200 million sold number. Next, 1994 year, the smartphone had reached 1.4 billion users. Following 2001 year, the Apple ipod had reached 350 million sold. Then, 2010 year, the Apple ipod had reached 100 million sold. However, in watching television/movie entertainment consumption consumers could have different choice, e.g. from 1975 year, consumers can choose VCR entertainment tapes to watch movies or television programs. Then, from 1995 year, consumers can choose DVD , following from 2007 year consumers can choose Netflix streaming recording cameras to record any movies or television programs to watch. It had reached 30 million subscription numbers. Following from 2012 year, entertainment consumers can choose Acreo FM internet signal to watch TV.

Anyway, the entertainment watching facilities development had been following this trend: Capacity from 1981 year, the capacity is broadband. then, from 1999 year, capacity is WiFi, it had 61% of households share market. Next, from 2001 year, the capacity is 3G technology, many people like to download any movies or TV programes to mobile phone to watch. Till to nowadays, the mobile phone capacity is improved to 4G technology, the mobile phone internet user number had reached 59 million current subscribers. So, it implies that many entertainment consumers like to use internet to download any movies or TV programs to mobile phones or laptops to watch.

It implies future internet development trend which can be used to entertainment industry. Hence, the future of television ought have implications for the component of a media company, when it applies internet technology to operate, such as IT service management, disaster recovery, digital content security, cloud etc. technological development.

Interactive advertising bureau (2013) indicated the devices used to view online television among US digital video viewers by type Mar 2013 1% of respondent(s), laptp had 58%, internet-connected TV had 47%, desktop has 39%, smartphone had 28%, tablet had 28% , ipodtouch had 14%.

Hence, it implied many entertainment consumers prefer to use laptop or internet connected to watch online TV television or movie in the future. These two channels will be the most popular online TV/movie entertainment channels in the future. Moreover, future internet technology development ought concentrate on improving it's speed, quality, performance to satisfy any laptop or internet connect TV entertainment consumers. Hence, future internet technology development ought concentrate on improving it's speed, quality, performance to satisfy any laptop or internet connect TV entertainment consumers.

● Internet innovative logistic industry communication development

What is future potential benefits and limitations of using internet to logistic operaters? The users pay attention to two new developments that may have a very large impact on the development of logistic has been pointed out, i.e. To the " internet of everything" and to the so-called fourth industrial revolution. Will internet be popular used by logistic transportation industry?

Nowadays, logistic transportation industry is facing challenges, factors include possibly quickest onset of transportation action, high efficiency as well as flexibility, whose main function is the maximinal adaptation to client needs, e.g. delivering any products or documents to any countries' clients in the most time and no any error to deliver the products or documents to the wrong receivers.

However, internet is increasingly influenced by the skillful management of modern technologies to assist delivering in efficiency. It is based on complex and comprehensive data sources, arising from and influencing the development of modern trends.

So, logistic industry needs have internet technology to help modern production, processing and logistics processes to satisfy the expectations of stakeholders.

The internet of things (IOT) is a new modes of communication, information connection between people and things, but in particular connection between objects (things). Hence, IOT management systems have a very wide range of applications and in terms of logistics, in a direct or in direct way many cover, among other, smart cities, intelligent industry, intelligent enterprises, intelligent buildings.

In the future, the group of significant trends in logistics include: big data/open data, cloud logistics; autonomous logistics, 3D printing, robotics and automation; internet of things; localization and local intelligence; wearable technology;augmented reality; low-cost sensor technology; crypto-currencies and crypto-payment. Hence, future logistics industry will need internet technology assistance to develop any businesses. For example, DHL logistic delivering firm, the first 6 trends belong to a group that will impact on : Firstly, big data/open data, it is a degree of digitization enterprise data can be shared in an unprecedented way. Integrated data streams in the supply chain of many logistic suppliers and open data sources have a very high potential for logistics operations, improvement of operational efficiency, full control over the suppl chain, assets and personal , the possibility of more accurate forecasts, and adjustment in real time.

Secondly, what is cloud logistics? It meets the challenges of complex diistributed , uncertains less predictable logistic conditions, reduction of the total cost of IT services (including the cost of installation, updatin , maintenance fees)., service risk minimization, faster and simply implementation, better reliability and security.

Thirdly, automonus logistic: It is stand-alone devices can be applied throughout. The supply chain from " the warehouse of the future" through auto-driven vehicles. Following the example of autopilots to unmanned supplies.

Fourthly, 3D printing is technology chnging the logistics by adding new manufacturing "mthods and possibl emergence of new market segments, such as the digital magazone.

Firthly, robotics and automation is the new generation of robots and automated solution will significantly better performance offers a serious alternative to manual labor, reducing time consuming actitivied aim. So, these will be internet is how applied to logistics industry trend in the future.

● Six key forces or " Drivers of change" impact on future online educational industry development

In the future, there will have to key drivers of change impact on future internet development, it includes : the internet and the physical world, artificial intelligence, cyber threats, the internet economy, networks, standards and interoperability and role of government. However, thesedrivers will have three areas of impact include: digital divides, personal freedoms and rights and media and society.

However, future internet technology will have these threats to influence its development. They include: civil society is seen as more important to raise needs, internet must remain user centric to raise competition, it is critical for individual safety and for the future internet economy, new thinking , new approaches and new models are needed across the board from internet policy to addressing digital divides from security approaches to economic regulation, multi-stakeholder needs will change increasing frequenty, internet users wil consider data collection and privacy in confidence.

In the future, artifical intelligent development will incresse internet needs in possible. The advent of artificial intelligence (AI) promises new opportunities, ranging from new services and breakthroughs in science to the augmentation of human intelligence in digitial world. For example, when there is significant hype about the possibilities hat (AI) may bring voices of concern to apply internet technology assistance. Hence, human must ensure that humans remain in the " internet and (AI) driver's technology combination ." Consequently, the hyperconnected internet economy that results will see traditionl industries to lead future new internet market leaders from around the globl driving innovation and entreprensurship. Hence, future internet and (AI) will be technological driven economy, it depends on how scientists improve their innovation.

However, scientists ethical consideration will be one important issue when they decide how to apply internet and (AI) technology. If they choose to apply them to war aspect, it is very horror matter to human's future safety. Hence, developing (AI) and internet technological countries need to consider scientist's behaviors in order to avoid war occurrence to cause human's death in future one day.

Hence, scientists ought follow this direction to develop internet technology. The future internet is needed to promise social development , economic prosperity and technologies that can ampify the best of humanity. But, it also brings about to solve challenges and questions to achieve to aim to raise human's social welfare or beneficial final direction.

What will be the certain factors to shape the future of the internet development? It includes as below: Social economic opportunity factor, it refers this ability how to connect people is essential to the internet's value as a platform for innovation, creativity and economic opportunity. How can the drivers of change encompass internet technological , economic, regulatory, security and network related challenges for the future internet . The drivers of change may include, such as how the internet economy development, what the role of government is, what the internet and physical world will shape, how internet assists artificial intelligent development, how to fight cyber threats, how networks standards and interoperable developments.

Future hospital, transportation, manufacturing etc. industries development factor how these industries develop, it will influence how internet needs. Because the rapid change will disrupt businesses and increse pressure on societies , particularly models and the nature of work will be profoundly changed to influence internet change needs. It is far from clear whether this internet technology driven assistance will favour existing internet platforms or bring greater competition and internet entrepreneurship.

How the internet economy will increase efficiencies, productivity and create new opportunities factor. Internet technology will reshape economies in ways stakeholders, and particularly governments may be ill-equipped to keep up with. And as technology drives automation, traditional jobs and the local economies that rely on them will be at risk. So, the future internet economy will depend on new approaches to skills and education. For example, traditional manufacturing sectors that were once relatively insulated must evolve to succeed in an increasingly connected internet economy. As devices and applicances are built to be network ready, the internet live needs us between manufacturing and manufacturing technological company increasing. Companies will need to adopt a technology mindset as they are from replacing parts to updating software to manufacture efficiently by internet and artificial intelligent technology assistance. Also, business is trying to protect against disruptions to their business models, for example, in the tussle between Google's automated cars and the automobile industry. For one, it's another application of sensor technology for the other , it's a change in mindset.

In the future, most widely used online services and platforms deeped their market position or face competition and possible displacement by new players? Could these internet companies face new competition from traditional industries as online in a world of IOT? Can internet platform be popular to be used for advertisements for businesses? (AI)/new generation of entrepreneurs like to use technology to solve local problems, reach global markets and drive innovation. Hence, online (internet) data search can be the best tool to help them to achieve their intention. I believe that it has not other technology can be replace internet to search lot of data in the short time within 10 years. Hence, internet of things (IOT) ought follo this direction to improve its quality to attract many clients. (entrepreneurs) to use this data serch service.

Moreover, artificial intelligence will be popular to be used. It will be beneficial to internet to be used. For example, a society completely based on data collection on the business. Humans lose some self-determination through automated choices by connected machines. So, our community across all stakeholder groups and regions believes that automation generated through data analytics technology will have greater influence on human behavior and decision making. So (AI) and internet can be cooperate to assist themselves to serve human. For example, (AI) could bring about a fundmental reshaping of decision-making as policy development's increasingly data driven. AS (AI) and automation drive significant structural change across industries, the nature of work will change. Many existing jobs may be displaced as (AI) moves beyond user data to changing how products and services are delivered from internet assistance. The communication between machine to machine increases pressures to cut costs and people are being replaced. This is only going to increase with time. There are economic benefits , but also challenges to employees.

Hence, if the internet platforms of today can become dominant across infrastructure, services and applications, user choice and control over their online experience, as well as availability and deliversity of information and content could be popular factor to influence internet economy. When search companies reach such a level of scalability, it is difficult for others to complete with them. For example, customers may find it is difficult to move from one provider or platform to another. This will cause in the loss of choice and constraints on innovation and lead to internet fragmentation. This is a trend to toward an ecosystem of users and developers, in which you can have the big winners or something similar to walled gardens. But there will always be some disruption tahta fragments this garden and creates a new paradigm. So , the reach and resources of internet platforms mean that startups will be acquired in their infancy, before they can disrupt the bigger players.

Will any internet companies replace Google, yahoo internet companies' services? This question is if smaller entrepreneurs are able to compare in an able to compete in an uncertain environment of investment analysis to the opportunities, these creates are ranging from new big data search service to the applied to intelligence in the digital world. So, artificial intelligence will be creative destruction. Many jobs will be also be eliminated by (AI) technological invention, but it can generate new jobs and jobs from internet , big data serch services assistance.

Future trend of mobile development influences to online education

Morgn Stanley reserch indicated that future past mobile vs. desttop internet user development trend within 5 years. Mobile internet users number was from 400 million 2007 year climbed up to 1,900 million 2015 year. Otherwise, desktop internet users number was from 1,000 millon 2007 year climbed up to 1,7500 million 2015 year. Hence, it implied that , although desktop internet user number was more than mobile internet user number in 2007 yer, but till to 2015 year,mobile internet user number was more than desktop internet user number. It reflect many people had accepted to apply mobile tool to do any internet search behaviors. It is possible that it will be popular to apply mobile tool to do internet search behaviors for long time in the future.

It brings this interesting question: Why do global internet users prefer to spend more time to apply mobile tools to do search behaviors from internet? I shall indicate that this technological teaching method example, such as how smart mobile phones and internet technolgy had changed the old phenomena of learning model in educational industry. The traditional phenomena of learning model was that teaching innovation means unit cost of teaching, success teaching evidence means number of teaching units deployed, every student can free access open teaching contents from internet channel of desktop tools, every student learning can be achieved every delivery and display from internet learning, every teacher training needs to achieve the first and last discussion to every student from internet online teaching tool.

Hence, many schools will accept to teach students from online teaching channel. Every student can turn on desktop to link to internet tool to learn at home conveniently. So, internet learning students do not need to go to schools, due to internet learning tool is similar to classroom to let teachers can apply internet channel to teach their students as well as students can listen their one teacher teach what in the same time when they open computer to link internet to see their teacher face and listen what who teach them after they log in their school website from internet channel conveniently. Hence, every group of students who can see teacher and listen what their teacher is teaching them in the same time after they turn on desktop to link to internet at home.

Some scientists also predict future mobie internet can be applied in educational and communication industries from 2020 year. Mobile internet can be applied to these aspects: education security, labguages, radio distributed systems, networking.

How can mobile internet be applied to children age education industry? I shall explain what what pocket school means. Pocketschool is not a name of device to be applied to different device for a different context, it is not a name software varies of open software contents, it is an initiative to help underrepresented children and migitate digital, education and economic divides. For a kind of mobile math learning game education method, it is a critical thinking math teaching method to children. Every child student can turn on mobile to learn how to apply simply math equation to calculation from mobile internet. Hence, future mobile internet tool won't only be applied to playing game aspect, it can be applied on education game aspect to let children to feel fun to learn from themselves. So, children can apply mobile internet to learn from device recognition to solve problem through collaborations, e.g. children cn apply moile internet tool to learn writting story ot telling story to increase learning internet or training to be authors. Mobile internet can also be applied to medical aspect, e.g. seeing any x ray images of brains , bones or any part of bodies, when medical photographs are delivered to download to the patient's mobile from the hospital easily.

In conclusion, in the future mobile internet will be popular used by mobile users and internet market must be expand to mobile tool market, instead of computer tool market.

1.1
How online educational growth raise educational qualities and education effective productivity.

Ha, Kim and Lee (2009) provided evidence to indicate that "using panel data covering from 1989 year to 2000 year in Japan, Korea and Taipei, China as the distance to the technology frontier narrows basis research and development (R&D) technological investment, i.e. highly online educational skilled labor (teachers) who can raise the higher educational qualities and educational productivities growth effect than only concentrates on development R&D technological investment , i.e. less investment on developing online educational skilled labor (teachers), more investment on developing research and development technological investment. They also provided evidence that the quality of online tertiary education has a significantly positive effect on the productivity of R&D, if the Asia countries have many students are educated to increase graduated student numbers to be supplied to societies to work by online education in the short term.

Nowadays, online education is commonly regarded as the most direct influence to people out of poverty owing to the tendency for employment opportunities especially for higher skilled workers to be created in Asia developing countries. In fact, raising online education productivity and online education quality is depended on the online student number demand and online teacher teaching quality of online education teacher human resource supply, which itself largely depends on investment in online education theoretical linkages between online educational productivity growth and online educational quality.

Generally, online education demand growth suggests that it depends on these factors, including the accumulation of economic, including online teacher human assets supply and the education method and education service performance. They depend on online education technological online classroom teaching progress, the online education efficiency which online education technological tools are being used. So, online education of online student demand and online teacher supply growth which emphasizes on the centrality of online teacher personal online teaching skill human capital for online teaching innovation and online educational technological tools in every online teaching progress from internet teaching channel.

However, the Asia online educational policy indicates that online educational productivity ineffectiveness, whose weaknesses incluce the lack of efficient online education production of online education new technologies development and online teacher al training of online education human capital development. So focusing on above these factors within the model rather than relying on external factors.

It seems the economists of supporting online educational productivity growth believe that improvements in online educational productivity are linked to a faster pace of online educational innovation and extra investment in online teacher human capital training in Asia countries, if any one of Asia countries expect to develop online education successfully. Also these economists support online education productivity growth, it emphasizes on the online education need for governments and private sector educational institutions and job markets for online educational tertiary students' demand as well as to innovate online educational knowledgeable of social economy to actively provide incentives for individual online education student to become inventive in any countries, such as Asia or Western countries. They also identify the central role of online learning and online teaching knowledge as determinant of online educational productivity growth. Hence, online educational productivity growth can predict positive externalities and spillover effects from development of a high valued-added online teaching and online learning knowledge to the online educational development and maintenance of a competitive advantage across the global online teaching industry.

How can online education performance and online educational method productivity influence the student number growth to Asia developing countries in the short term? In fact, to achieve successful online teaching human capital includes different online subjects, online teaching methods and online teacher performance or personal teaching qualities these factors. The main focus of the present study is on how to design online subjects and how to apply online educational tools to teach online students and every online teacher how to teacher whose students from internet channel.

The analysis stresses the distination between the quality and quantity of online education is measured by years of attainment at various levels and the quality measured by scores on internationally comparable examinations, e.g. China online education and Korea online education student examination result comparision.

A key feature of these models is a theory of online teaching technological progress, viewed as a online teaching process whereby purposeful research and application lead over time to new and better online education productivity and educational performance as well as methods of online teaching to every online online educational subject.

The recent online education growth models are useful for understanding why advanced economies and the world is as whole, can continue to grow in the long run despite the workings of diminishing returns in the accumulation of online educational physical, e.g. internet speed and performance quality and online teacher human capital training.

For example, these countries include, e.g. America, England which are observed to be rich and high tend also to be those that have high long run target levels of per high capita output in a setting that includes online teacher human capital supply and online educational technological change. So online education is also essential to raise online education teacher labour knowledge and online education training and internet technological online education level innovation to assist developed countries, e.g. USA, UK , to raise online subject number productivity raising to achieve global online education industy economic growth.

So, the developed or developing countries' both government policies and online education institutions need to concern their national online student demand population to arrange the different primary, secondary and tertiary online educational policy to educate to develop whose online students to develop different professional and knowledgeable and skillful abilities to already develop their careers in different nature of jobs to enter their societies to work nowadays in the short time. So, online education can solve short term graduated supply challenge to every country.

However, if we were the identify how online education contributes to cause global online education economic growth in any Asia developing countries. We need to compare states that have a similar distance to the frontier and yet choose difference pattern of investment in online education development and new teaching method.

For example, building a new online education school for a online research university, the process is when a vacancy arises on an committee that controls expenditure. Because governments and online universities need to concern what the labour market demand, so the research online university can decide prefer to choose what kinds of online subjects to be taught to its potential online students, e.g. medical or architect or law or engineering or business or social science, computer science etc. different online subjects among of them subjects, which online subjects will be chosen to be taught to its potential online students preferably. So, the job demand market research is very important because it can help the online research university to choose what the preferable online subjects will be demanded to supply to the labour market increasing in any one of Asia developing countries within future three or five years.

Online education growth have emphasised the role of online teacher human capital which may affect global online education industry economic growth. Online teacher (Human capital) is as an extra input in the aggregate production function, where the output of the means economy is a direct function of both factor inputs: Online classroom and online educational tools (physical capital), online teacher (labor and human capital). However, internet online education technologies can raise innovate capacity of online educational industry through developing new ideas. So, online education was seemed that it could be raised graduated students' abilities to raise productivity to any one of Asia developing countries and to solve graduated shortage challenge by high technological skill in the future long term.

1.2 Why computer information technology and internet will be future popular teaching method.

In the beginning, I shall indicate my opinions to explain why computer and internet technology will be the best tool to solve any educational challenges as well as I shall recommend how any education organizations can apply this new technology to educate students effectively and efficiently.

In generaly, educators think that education means considerably more than just teaching a student to read, write and numbers only. However, nowadays, computers, the internet nd advanced electronic are becoming essential in everyday life and have changes the way information is gathered. So, it brings these questions such as, how is this new technology utilized and managed by teachers to solve any teaching challenges more easily? Will this new technology have an important role to play in widening the resource and knowledge base for all students?

Technology affects the way teachers teach and student learn. To make the best use of information technology, schools need a workable plan to fully integrate in all aspects enhance their learning. So, if a school doesn't have a clear plan of how and why it wishes to implement information technology (IT), then it runs the risk of wasting money. The important reason why I believe internet will be one new technological teaching method to any universities because internet has reach the mature and popular stage to let any university students accept to use this method to learn in the future.

In schools today, nearly all classrooms have access to a computer. However, many schools mistake this as incorporating information technology into the curriculum. School staff need to research what IT is available and what would best serve the school's purpose, not simply purchase the latest equipment. There should be a policy stating how IT is going to assist pupil's development and what teachers want pupils to achieve. Staff members need to be clear about what they want IT to do for them before who can start incorporating in into their lessons.

So, the only way information technology is going to be useful to schools is if all staff members are well-informed and fully supported absolutely. It is the principal's responsibility and should be part of the school's plan to ensure that all staff are consulted about the changes and that the change is carefully organized. It seems that any universities need to spend time to prepare how to change to adopt this IT and internet new technological educational method from traditional lecturer face-to-face oral teaching method if which expect future student emotion and teaching challenges will be solve successfully. For example, some teachers may be especially learnt if who have not had much experience with computers by computer professionals teaching , so computer training teachers are essential in implementing IT into the school curriculum. Staff members must feel involved in the process of acquiring technology and in learning how to operate it, in order for them to increase their confidence in using IT as a curriculum tool. So, primary and secondary teachers , even university tutors are only going to be able to incorporate IT into their lessons if they are potential users themselves.

In addition, teachers need to be aware that IT within the classroom is extremely flexible, but that they need to plan what purpose IT serves in eaach lesson. The skills of a student learning are the important part of any lesson, and it is the same with technology. It needs to be used and understood in all subjects in the same way as the ability to read is necessary for all subjects and must be used across the curriculum in the same way that pen and pencil are used in most subject areas in any primary schools, secondary schools, even universities.

Anyway, the best way to plan the use of IT in the classroom will be approached it as simply a learning tool that is more advanced and more existing and exciting than the traditional pen and paper in any primary and secondary schools and universities in the future. The most important reason, IT educational method will attract many students to choose the school to study. Because internet had reached the mature stage and it will be one popular teaching acceptance tool to any students. Thus, it is vitually important for students to be taught the strategies for using IT to let students aware that the contexts in which their traditonal pen and pencil learning and writing method will be changed to be internet and IT typing and learning method as well as teachers need to know what the appropriate use of IT is and what is not when it is important that students learn to use IT effectively. However, I shall indicate these educational challenges will cause and how IT tool will solve as below:

Educational subject development challenge

USA science and engineering subject future challenge

Nowadays, US played a critical role in establishing leadership in science and engineering (S&E) education aspect, however, the next generation of scientists will need to solve these science and engineering subject educational challenge. For example, how to ensure future generations continue to reap the benefits of fundamental S&E research. They need to give big ideas of what benefits can be given to the next generation students. Such as US country science and engineering research will lose serious and non-value if it doesn't ensure what benefits can be given to the next generation. So, IT educational method can be attempted to solve this science and engineering subject educatonal challenge, due to this subject students need to often to do research and experiment to prepare to finish their assignments. Internet will be one useful tool to help students to gather any science and engineering datas to finish their assignment easily. So, computers and internet must need

need to be used by students in any school classrooms.

The catalyze interest and investment in fundamental (S&E) research which needs the basis for discovery, invention and innovation benefits. They are meant to define a set of cutting-edge research agendas and processes that are uniquely suited for (S&E)'s broad portfolio of investment and will require collaborations with industry, private foundations, other agencies, science academies and societies and universities.

On US (S&E) student numbers learning difficulty aspect, how to solve some of the most pressing problems the world faces as well as lead to discoveries not yet known to our (S&E) education, such as US development (S&E) education? For example, US is experiencing a period of significant demographic shifts , the Census Bureau projects that by 2050 year, minorities will comprise 53% of the population.

Nowadays, it has approximately 30% of people are now working in (S&E) are minorities. To maintain US leadership in science, the nation must address the challenge of broadening participation for the next generation. So, to solve the one (S&E) student numbers shortage common problem. It will develop scalable ways to educate the potential among traditionally underrepresented groups, including women. African Americans, native Americans, persons with disabilities, people from rural areas and people of low socioeconomic status. Thus, US (S&E) student numbers can be the next generation (S&E) student numbers shortage problem gap or take advantage of new opportunities. US universities will need to teach the uneducated and less computer and internet knowledge African Americans, native Americans, persons with disabilites, people from rural aread and people of low socioeconomic staus science and engineering students how to use internet to gather data from computers to prepare their learning easily in the future.

On US (S&E) teacher teaching challenge aspect, imagine researchers being able to precisely foresee future characteristics of biological organisms, human disease risk, drug therapy response, food crop yields and environmental remediation to name just a few. Nature is full of diverse species in all shapes, colors and sizes. Each with characteristics resulting from a complex interaction of genetics and the environment. For example, the universally recognized biggest gap in biological knowledge is their inability to predict an organism's observable characteristics, its phenotype from what we know about its genetics and environment. Many factors influence the traits in an organism, making this prediction is extreme complex. This biological educational challenge will require research across biology, computer science, mathematics, behavioral sciences and engineering. This initiative understanding the rules of life predicting phenotype will include research in data integration analysis, modeling and informatics techniques. So, US science and engineering teachers need to learn how to apply internet to raise teaching quality to teach their students more easily and effectively and efficiently in classroom.

I recommend an online platform of data tools for large scale analysis of complex biological problems will be one suitable tool to be used for educational aim in the future. I also recommend to apply internet teaching toole to change future school science and engineering experiment work place to carrying on any science and engineering experimenting in school laboratories. It will require a changing future school experiment work force, making (S&E) education and lifelong learning important priorities. We need have a unique opportunity to actively shape the development and use of techniques to improve the quality of experiment work when also increasing productivity and economics growth in manufacturing and in service sectors, such as healthcare and education from internet technology. For example, (S&E) activities rely increasingly on infrastructure that is diverse in space, cost and implementation time , everything from major observatories to nationwide sensor networks to smaller experiments from internet educational tool.

The (S&E) education major challenge is that there many important potential experiments and facilities that fall between these amounts; this gap results in missed opportunities that leave essential science undone. The long term consequences of that neglect will be profound for science as well as for US action's economy, security and competitiveness. So, US universities science and engineering lecturers will need a new approach to research in infrastructure. One more dynamic and flexible internet teaching tool will be in response to this new reality in the future.

The eduational method challenges to higher education engineering lecturers

High education (HE) has become more globalized and is slowly changing from being teacher-centered to study-centered. Industry is ever more demanding of graduates' employability and value. Degree programs are required to address the learning outcomes their graduates should attain (including : discipline and contextual knowledge, practice knowledge and skills and personal and professional attributes).

What challenges to higher education engineering lecturers meet? For example, teaching core engineering concepts to assist student engineers to learn how to apply them to solve a problem sometimes supplemented with placements. This is traditional teaching method challenge, so engineering lecturers need to change to apply technological educational method to let engineering students to feel learning more easily. However, new technological teaching method is popular to be applied to lecturers, but it also encounter difficulty, such as students need to understand e.g. risk, critical thinking, business acumen, social desirability of designs and how to adapt their role in innovation to attract student engineers' attention.

How to meet demand for engineering graduates? High education is growing into engineering qualifications, essential to attractive, creative, enthusiastic, engaged students from all backgrounds.

Thus, higher education engineering lecturers are hoped to train engineering students who can have self-directed learning, transferable skills development. So, higher education engineering lecturer role of teacher is as an educator and learning facilitator. For example, engineering education needs apply new technological educational innovation. Innovation in engineering education can ensure transform students into graduates who are well prepared for future engineering practice, exploits new science and technology is responsive to change socio-economic and environmental contexts. Because nowadays, engineers are hoped creative, innovation ready, entrepreneurial, critically thinking , socially responsible engineers.

Thus, higher education engineering lecturers need have innovation mind to arrange how to gather data to prepare each lesson to teach engineering students from internet , such as engineering lecturers disciplinarily with increasing use of problem and project based learning, group learning and assessment, authentic workplace learning and research –based /enquiry learning. It seems future lectures need to own innovation and critically thinking mind. Then, who can train students to own the same mind to learn more easily and independently from internet assistance.

What are the limites to the future of higher educational opportunities for India ?

Nowadays, India's education system is as one of the world's largest, has been studied and reflected on through academic papers, used as a case study and been the subject of many renowned books. This is a traditional India educational models. The educational innovation and change are required and understanding that change will be essential to India education system because India's demographic trend means it will soon over take China as the world's largest population. Thus, India is encountering population growth challenge to cause shortage of school supply to students to study. The Indian higher education system is facing on challenge is being driven by economic and demographic change by 2020 year. India will be the world's third largest economy with a correspondingly rapid growth in the size of its middle classes. Currently , over 50% of India population is under 25 years old by 2020 year . India will outpace China as the country with the largest tertiary age population.

Thus, Indian higher education is facing with four broad challenges, such as:

The supply –demand gap challenge: BY 2020 year, the Indian government aims to achieve 30% gross enrolment, which will mean providing to million university places, an increases of 14 million in six years.

The low quality of teaching and learning challenge: Shortage of faculty , poor quality teaching, outdated curricular, lack of accountability and quality assurance and separation of research and teaching.

Constraints on research and innovation challenge: With a very low level of PHD enrolment. India does not have enough high quality researchers, there are less opportunities for interdisciplinary and multidisciplinary working, lack or early stage research experience, a weak ecosystem for innovation and low levels of industry engagement.

Uneven growth and access to opportunity challenge: Socially access to higher education is uneven with inequalities in enrolment areas population groups and geographies.

Thus, India government needs to reform educational policy, but many predict higher education leader academics and policy makers in India to explore their views on what the future holds for them and link to collaborate with the UK. For example, India educational organizations can co-operate with UK, USA etc. developed countries' famous and successful educational institutes to apply internet to teach India students by distance learning method. If India students had any learning challenges , who can send their questions to enquire these overseas countries' lecturers to get feebacks easily by email channel. Also, India teachers can send email with overseas developed countries' teachers to discuss different teaching methods easily.

Thus, key challenges are facing the system includes educational quality assurance, credit transfer system; between higher education and vocational skills solution method include promoting higher education and vocational skills stream and teacher training in higher education, change college education method to improve the quality of teaching and learning, private educational business sector will continue to grow , but for profit high education is unlikely to be sanctioned soon international cooperating with UK institutions to make the most of educational opportunities and foreign education providers need to take a long term view and build closer multi -dimensional relationship with Indian institutions.

Education challenges of the global science students in 21 St century

The national assessment of educational progress indicated a scale of 1 to 300 for reporting performance in science. Form 1996 year to 2005 year, the national average 4th grade science score increased from 147 to 151 , but there was no measurable change in the 8th grade score, and the 12th grade score actually decreased from 150 in 1996 year to 147 in 2005 year. Digest of education statistics 2010 (pg.2, pg. 63). It brings this question: What factors cause global science students whose scores can not raise in the 8th grade as well as the 12th grade score actually decreases from 1996 to 2005 year in common.

The performance data showed global middle school and high school science students on an average are performing around the 50 percentage. The OECD (2009) program showed that international student assessment evaluates the quality , equity and efficiency of school system in some 70 countries that together, make up nine-tenths of the world economy. Its tests are designed to find out whether science students can use what who have learned in schools and apply their knowledge to real life situations and problems. It's test result show countries where which stand in relation to other countries and how effective which educate their students. Thus, it implies global science students' learning methods and teachers' educational method will have close relationship to influence global science student individual score performance and learning performance. It brings this question: Can technological education method improve science students' learn methods and raise quality of teachers' educational method?

However, global science students will feel challenges to learn science. The reasons include, such as an individual learning level, because of an increasingly learning world learning competition will influence overseas university student enrollment or even from across the student himself/herself country but from across the world. As a society, if it's universities or secondary schools are not able to develop a next generation that is capable of solving the pressing problems of human will face in many areas, including climate change, social and economic inequality and dwindling natural and energy resources. It is therefore difficult to figure not now schools can address the issue of how to evaluate the performance of our science students.

I recommend how to apply internet educational method to solve these challenges, such as:

The first method is that global science teachers, parents and country leaders in different countries government, business and academic need to consider how earth science challenges, such as global climate changing, food shortage, water and air pollution etc. problems, due to globalization and advances in technology influence. So, they can apply internet to encourage science students to know how these above natural disasters causes from online learning. So, online learning method can influence science students to consider these earth warming result to raise their interest to be proficient in creativity, critical , thinking and communication of ability to achieve their best learning performance in possible in the future.

The second method is that I think we can meet objective by designing a online learning environment around networked learning technologies , a project based learning approach and online and science student in person real natural environment traveling method with school science teachers together on Saturday and Sunday non-school days. Before science students can find or gather any natural science related data to prepare to assist whose studying more easily out classrooms from internet , then their science teachers can bring them to visit natural environment, such as natural parks or forests to investigate different plants, animals and natural lands themselves to learn more easily as well as their visiting the country real natural environment both, the science teachers can let science students to absorb what the actual natural challenges are actually occurring. Thus, science students need to gather data and learn how these natural disaster causes from internet learning methods, due to interent learning method will raise many global science student individual interest to learn science subject in short time effectively.

The trend of challenges of educational development of the 21st century global society

The 21st century educational skills became known as critical thinking, communication, collaboration and creativity. So, every individual student is needed own ability to solve any learning challenges. In the global manufacturing economies that existed 50 years ago, students need own reading, writing and calculation ability to learn easily, even how to gather useful data to prepare to study from internet channel. Because, in modern world, students must be proficient communicators, creators, critical thinkers and collaborators and students need have effort to study these subject areas, including foreign languages, the arts, geography, science, law, business and social studies etc. subjects. It seems internet channel is the sole learning method to let any subject students to gather data to prepare their learning more easily in the short time.

As the same time, due to workforce skills and demands have changed dramatically in the last twenty years, e.g. many labor manufacturing method had change to new technological manufacturing method., even, labor service job will also change to artificical intelligence service job as soon as possible. Moreover, global employers need to employ employees who need have a rapid increase in jobs involving non-routine, analytic and interactive communication skills. Thus, it causes today's job market requires competencies , such as critical thinking and the ability to interact with the company employees from many different cultural backgrounds employee working environment. Thus, students need own these critical thinking and excellent communication skills to prepare to work in society. It seems any country's schools need to teach students these skills to prepare to work in societies. It brings this question: Can internet channel attract students to learn how to use critical thinking mind and attitude to solve their learning difficulty and future working difficulty in any working environment easily?

To answer this question, we need to know what the critical thinking is. Critical thinking and problem solving can be defined as: Using various types of reasoning (inductive, deductive etc.) as appropriate to the situation , using systems thinking to analyze how parts of a whole interact with each other to produce overall outcomes in complex systems; making judgements and decisions in effectively analyzed and evaluated evidence, arguments, claims and belief, analyzing and evaluating major alternative points of view, synthesizing and making connections between information and arguments, interpreting information and drawing conclusion based on the best analysis, reflecting critically on learning experiences of unfamiliar problems in both conventional and innovative ways and identifying and asking significant questions that clarifying various points of view and leading to better solutions (Catalina Foothills School District). Thus, if the university student owned these abilities to learn. I believe that who must feel not difficulties to learn.

Then, it brings this question: How critical thinking and problem solving can be integrated into classroom teaching and learning across a variety of grade levels and disciplines. For art subject student example, music students individually articulate different ways to interpret the same musical passage. Students then compare the various interpretations and determine which one is most effective, taking into account age-appropriate considerations, such as the style of the music. For another world languages student example , with the job title omitted , students read various job/ career advertisements and then match the appropriate job title to the ad. Students are divided into groups. Each group is asked to investigate 3 to 5 different career/job sites and identify the jobs and careers that are in high demand in a particular city, region or country. Then, students can present their findings of the most suitable world languages learning method to the class. Next, for science students example, who need to research how the physical and chemical properties of different natural and human designed materials affect their decomposition under various conditions. So, I recommend students can apply internet to gather data to compare their findings to the material evidence used by scientists to reconstruct the lives of past cultures, as well as create a map of their classroom as a future written descriptions of artifacts and what who imply about the cultures, discovered by scientists. So, the science students can be trained to learn how to apply critical thinking to plan and conduct scientific investigations and write detailed explanations based on their evidence when they often apply internet to gather data to compare their findings to the material evidence used by scientists to make judgement to prepare their learning in every lesson.

Thus, the owned critical thinking skillful science students who can compare their explanations to those made by scientists and relate them to their own understandings of the natural and designed world more easily. Finally for social studies students example, in groups , students explore how selected societies for fuel (e.g. England's use of its forests at the beginning of the industrial revolution) and the economic impact of that use. The owned critical thinking skillful social studies students will choose to use videoconference by internet oral communication channel (e.g. www.skp.com) to collect information from relevant government officials about the use of corn for biofuel instead of food and analyze the environmental and economic implications of this use. For example, after they gather data to find any scientific evidences from internet channel. Then, they can choose to use sound reasoning and relevant scientific evidence examples, who can also analyze the historical evolution of a contemporary public policy issue, place it within a cultural and historical context, and use a online digital publishing tool to report the work from internet channel. In conclusion, above of these learning behaviors, which are the owned critical thinking or skillful students who will choose to decide to do these learning behaviors habitually from internet channel. Also, I feel global schools specially, universities and secondary schools ought train whose students to learn how to use internet channel to gather data to do critical thinking to solve any learning problems easily.

Future science, technology, engineering and mathematics students' learning challenges

Science, technology, engineering and mathematics will be popular subjects to any developed countries, such as US, UK, Japan as well as developing countries, such as China, India, Hong Kong, Korea growth subjects, even global economic competitiveness and the demand of these subject students will increase to study these subjects in US, even global. Because global many employers will increase demand these qualified workers, due to these qualified workers will have shortage of numbers to supply to global employment market. It trends in k-12 and higher education science and math. Also, preparation coupled with demographic and labor supply trends point to a serious quality of educational worker challenge. Such as, global nations need to increase the supply and quality of knowledge workers whose specialized skills to enable them to work productivity within technology industries and occupations in global. It will bring this question: Can internet technology can raise these Science, technology, engineering and mathematics subjects of teachers' quality of teaching level?

Nowadays, US Department of labor already investing about $14 billion one year in the nation's workforce system and in increasing the science, technology, engineering and math. students' skills and education. So, how to raise student's individual skills to US competitiveness and growth to science, technology , engineering and math. subjects that will be US educational development challenge. Opinion leaders and the publish board agree that education in math. and science is critical to the nation's future success. According to a recent educational testing service survey, it indicated 61% of opinion leaders and 40% of the general publish identify math, science, and technology skills will be the most important ingredients in the nation's strategy to compete in the global economy (Zinth 2006).

Thus, in US , the science, technology, engineering and math. students' multi-faceted education and workforce challenge include: Many students never feel studying these subjects easily, because of inadequate preparation in math. and science or poor teacher quality in their K-12 education systems(ACT 2006). Many who are academically qualified for postsecondary studies in science and math. fields of both the two and four year levels don't pursue those programs. The might be dissuaded by disappointing curricula and course of study, relatively low salary in these professional (American Association Of State College And Universities 2005).

In conclusion, it is the right time US , even global science, technology, engineering and math. subjects teachers can attempt to learn how to apply internet to teach their students in classroom to let them to feel to learn these subjects effectively and easily.

Future trends in K-12 education challenges

In the future, the majority of trends in K-12 education will use technology , such as cloud computing, mobile learning, learning analytics, open content, remote or virtual laboratories are directly related to improved student learning. However, it will have difficulty to achieve technology education to k-12. Because these young students need time to learn how to apply different computer software or high technology equipment to learn. Moreover, the changing uses of technology require that teachers also change their methods of instruction.

Online cloud computing, mobile learning , virtual laboratories, learning analytics, open content and remote technological learning methods which aim to achieve the studying or learning plan to encourage students can direct their own learning. As a result, teachers must shift from being holders and distributors of knowledge to becoming instructional facilitators who encourage students to direct their own learning.

Thus, the challenges of technological education will need to achieve how to direct students feel easy to use technological tools to learn conveniently. Several tools are available to support teachers. Such as social learning networks, e-portfolios and cloud computing allow teachers virtually connect and encourage discussion about best practice among teachers. For cloud computing education tool example, it comprises internet-based tools that don't live on an individual device. This flexibility allow for access to materials stored and the cloud at any location. Students can access homework assignments, readings and support materials anywhere, who can connect with the cloud.

Commonly used examples of cloud computing sharing devices are drop box and google drive. Also, cloud computing is popular in distance learning programs for obvious reasons. There are three categories of cloud computing that may be useful to k-12 educators (Nagel, D. 2013) indicated it includes infrastructure -as-a-service (i.e. virtualization). This category describes scalable virtual machines, bandwidth and storage capacities, platform-as-a-service (Pass). This category describes the environment in which the development and delivery of applications occurs and software-as-a-service (psas). This category describes software that is created for a specific organization's unique needs. Thus, k-12 students need to spend time to learn what are these category difference, then who can choose to use what may or method to use cloud computing to learn more easily in four years.

So, it brings this question: Why k-12 students need to apply cloud computing to learn. The reason is mobile technologies have also attracted the attention of high profile educational publishers, such as person, e-books, e-magazines publishers and interactive textbook have optimized for mobile platforms and devices and can easily replace heavier traditional textbooks. It also allow children to interact with material using simple fingers swipes and pinches, which eliminates the need for detailed instructions. It seems it has one day detailed instructions and electronic books will be popular to let any young students to accept to study, such as primary and high school and university students who can learn from computers or mobiles in future one day. Thus, it is the right time k-12 students to learn how to apply technology to learn.

Anyway, distance or distributed e-learning education is one of the most complex issues facing higher education institutions today. However, there are much challenge to education k-12 students by learning. How can teachers teach k-12students by distance education, e-learning or distributed learning method to achieve the effective learn outcome? Is it an extensive of the k-12 classroom or replacement leave? Distance learning is a subject of distributed learning, focusing on k-12 students who may be separated in time and space from their pears and the instructor. Distributed learning can occur either on or off campus, providing k-12 students with greater flexibility and eliminating time as a barrier to learning, campus or online. There are many implications of technology into education , i.e. in making learning distributed . So, the challenge indicates k-12 students to learn how to allocate time to learn from distance learning technology method. For example, eating time, sleeping time, doing homework time and learning time allocation. Teachers need teach students how to arrange and allocate time to learn or sleep or do homwork effectively and easily.

1.3 Distance learning online education challenges

Common assumptions about higher education include: schools know the student profile and learner preferences for learning and service delivery, student credit hours and full time equivalents are relevant units of measure in distributed education, completion of the curriculum is the measure of competency, traditional institutional models (e.g. for classroom instruction, governance and financing) will be successful in an e-learning educational method, higher education must provide all components of the educational process (e.g. content, curriculum, services and credentialing), external providers of educational services (e.g. courses or tutoring from an internet start-up) are bad or of lower quality than educational institutions, quality is better in a not-for-profit educational organization than in a for profit one, high education will be driven out low quality from bad online education influence, distributed learning is a variable option for all post-secondary education institutions, the faculty member is the focal point od the learning process.

So,All higher education institutions must develop their own distributed learning programs. Although, these assumptions characteristic are good, but which may not all apply to distance distributed learning. Some educational organizations have either inadequate or inappropriate for distributed learning. For example, the nation of credit for seat time has sustained current model of higher education, but will it suffice for a future represented by distributed learning?

However, technological education will bring these negative influences to students. What are the challenges in influence students psychology from information age mind set? When students often use computer or laptop to learning , constant connectivity, they will reduce time to communicate or make close relationship with whose friends and family at any time and from any place. Then, every online learning student behavior and value will be influences, such as: computers aren't technology only. It is whose part of life, the internet is better than TV reality is no longer real, doing is more important than knowing, trial-and-error, experimentation is preferable to logic , multitasking is a way of life, typing is preferable to handwriting, staying online learning connected is essential every day.

There is zero tolerance for online on-line learning time delays. Thus, the way, schools must organize their educational institutions to change educational method to achieve online learning time and private entertainment time to be balances to every student. Although, online education can give convenient and fast speed to gather information benefits to young students to study. But, educators need to consider these online education challenges which, online educational students will encounter , such as : What kind of support to faculty needs to develop engaging and empowering online environment? Are educators using the unique capabilities of the web to make learning environments engaging and effective? Do educators know which students will learn best of a distance and those for whom it is a poor choice? Thus, it brings this question: Does distributed learning support a specific strategic goal for the educational institutions or is the rationale?

To gain the commitment of all those who must support a major initiative (board , executive cabinet, faculty, teaching staff etc.) , it is important to articulate clearly the strategic goals behind the institution's interest in distributed learning. For example, which is the institution's commitment to educational access? Would distributed education enhance the fulfilment of that goal? Will it seem inconsistent with policies on selectivity and/or the importance of the residential experience? Does distributed education complement educational institution's mission, culture and historic strengths? Do the institutions have clear rationale for distributed eduaction?

Corporate learners work for corporations and are seeking education to maintain or the employing corporation and not by the individual acting alone. Professional enhancement learners are seeking to advance careers or shift careers. They are working adults who make the educational purchasing decision on their own.

Degree-completion adult learners are working to complete a degree at an older age . They frequently are working adults who must balance work and family needs with their educational goals. College experience learners are preparing for life , e.g. the traditional students. This segment includes many of the 18 to 24 year old residential college students for whom the coming age process is almost as important as academic achievement. Finally, I shall suggest pre-college (k-12) learners are interested in doing degree level work prior to the completion of high school. This learner age segment may be interested and is more acceptable in getting studying to compare other learnerage segment from internet learning channel.

TWO

THE RELATIONSHIP BETWEEN ONLINE TEACHER HUMAN CAPITAL TEACHING METHOD AND GRADUATED STUDENT NUMBER GROWTH

Nowadays, high education (HE) has become more globalized and is slowly changing from being teacher-centered to study-centered. So, online method of education Industry is ever more demanding of graduates' employability and value. Online degree programs are required to address the learning outcomes their graduates should attain (including : discipline and contextual knowledge, practice knowledge and skills and personal and professional attributes).

However, any countries' schools can choose either teaching students in classroom or online teaching channels. The first channel is that classroom teaching method when teachers human capital who need to go to classroom to teach whose students face to face, which is a direct teacher personal input in the teaching production function and the second channel is that online teaching method when the teacher, human capital affects the technology parameter to teach whose students when whose students turn on whose computer at home. The result establishes a long run online classroom teaching relationship between the online teacher and online students.

A well online educated labour force appears to significantly influence the online graduate number growth both as a factor in the online learning production function and through total factor of online learning communication productivity. With its large resources of online teacher human and natural online learning and teaching tool resources, the potential to build a prosperous online learning economy to reduce the poverty students who have not afford to pay expensive school fee to go to school to study, due to who can choose to pay less school fee to online study significantly as well as to provide the onlineeducation services to its population online learning needs.

As the Asia developing countries, e.g. China or Korea, which are poor countries past years, which need foreign investors' different businesses development in their countries. So, themselves online education need is commonly regarded as the most direct avenue to rescue a substantial number of online learning people out of poverty since there is likely to be more employment opportunities and higher wages for skilled workers.

Furthermore, online education can enable children's attitudes and assists them to grow up with social values that are more benefitical to their nations and themselves because these developing countries children can pay less school fee to learn how to apply high technology to learn to raise their knowledge level in the short term from internet channel.

Moreover, they can be rapid to graduate, due to online learning do not need them to spend much time to go to school often. So, they can spend much time to gather data to do homework from internet channel, and they can send email to enquire whose teacher when they feel difficult to learn and teacher can give feedback to let whose students to know their answers from email immediately from internet channel. In long term, it is possible that online education and learning method can let many poor students have chance to study in order to cause the graduated student number increases to solve the graduate shortage supply challenge to societies in the long term online education development.

The theoretical basis of online education on online graduated number growth is rooted in the endogenous growth theory. Endogenous growth economists believe that improvements in online education productivity can be linked to a faster pace of innovation and extra investment in online teacher human capital. Engogenous growth theorists argue the need for government and private sector online teaching institutions and online education markets which need to innovate and provide incentives for online learning student individuals to be inventive to encourage to learn from internet channel at home. There is also a central role for online learning technological knowledge as a determinant of online learning economic growth theory can predict positive online learning externalities and spill over effects from development of a high valued-added online learning knowledge economy which is able to develop and maintain a competitive advantage in online education growth industries in the global online learning economy. Nowadays, online education at high and low standard of living countries through imparting general online student personal learning attitudes and discipline and special online learning skills necessary for a variety of online learning places. Online learning contirbutes to online ecommerce economic growth by improving and reducing fertility and possibly by contributing to the online learning countries' political stability to different developing or developed both countries.

The major importance of the online educational system to any online teaching labor market would depend majority in ability to produce a literate, disciplines, flexible online teaching labor force via high online teaching quality of education. Consequently, with online education ecommerce economic development new online learning technology is applied to online teaching production with results in an increase in the demand for any related to online education service workers to raise more job opportunities in high online technological industry and better online education service.

In the developing countries, e.g. China, Korea, rich individuals allocate labor time not only for their own production and knowledge accumulation, but also train the poor individuals. In the past, some economists estimated a model of online education economic growth and online teacher human capital accumulation based on a sample of developing countries, e.g. China, Korea etc. are not a stable or mature stage of online education development. Their result revealed that the increase in the primary and secondary countries to an increase in online school productivity.

Economists indicate that online teacher human capital acccumulation rates are affected by demographic variables. So, these Asia countries need to spend time to train many teachers to learn how to apply internet to teach students in order to raise their online education performance and education quality. For example, they need establish that an increase in life expectancy at birth brings about an increase online learning needs in online learning secondary and tertiary education when a decrease in the dependence rate of online learning negatively affects secondary education. It aims to let secondary students believe online learning is more attractive and more raising their learning ability to compare with traditional classroom learning method.

2.1

Can online teaching can raise graduated student number?

The GDP per unit of online teacher labor input should be related to the share of online teacher labor of a particular type (online graduated student number and online education worker number at different qualification levels) weighted by the average online teacher human capital of the specific subject of online teaching worker (captured by the relative online teacher wages of different subjects of online teacher labor input). It seems measure of the relationship between online education service supplier and online teacher number and the online graduated student number can be quantified clearing to developing Asia any countries.

In past, the EUKLEMS project indicated key findings of 15 developed countries for one economic report: GDP per employment hour increased from 1992 year to 2005 year, the highest annual average percentage change was in Finland (2.7%), Japan (2.5%) and the UK (2.4%). These countries had the lowest level of GDP per employment hour in 1982 year, when the period considered the Netherlands and the USA had the highest GDP employment hour. Also it indicated the share of employment with tertiary education also increased from 1982 year to 2005 year in all countries. The highest annual average percentage change was in Australia (5%) followed by the UK (4.9%). Both of these countries had relatively low shares of employment with tertiary education in 1982 year at 6%, compared with 22.1% in the USA and 18.7% in Finland.

The large increased closed the gap, but the USA and Finland still had higher employment shares with tertiary education than Australia and the UK in 2005 year. The economic report also indicatd that a 1% increase in the share of the workforce with a university degree raises the level of long run productivity by 0.2%-0.5%. So, it implied the traditional classroom education and student graduated student number productivity has close relationship to developed countries also. However, the online education economic benefits will be more popular to raise graduate student number more than the traditional classromm graduate student number, both to the online learning individual student and to the wider online learning economy of a university online education degree with clearly depend on the online teaching method and online teaching course quality and online teacher skills to developing and developed countries both. So, improvement in online educational outcomes have been widely recognised as essential in enhancing online learning growth in both developed and developing countries. In fact, online education is acquire by online learning student individuals provide social returns at the macroeconomic level and addition indirect benefits to online education ecommerce economic growth.

For India online education development example, nowadays, India's education system is as one of the world's largest, has been studied and reflected on through academic papers, used as a case study and been the subject of many renowned books. This is a traditional India educational models. The educational innovation and change are required and understanding that change will be essential to India education system because India's demographic trend means it will soon over take China as the world's largest population. Thus, India is encountering population growth challenge to cause shortage of school supply to students to study. The Indian higher education system is facing on challenge is being driven by economic and demographic change by 2020 year. India will be the world's third largest economy with a correspondingly rapid growth in the size of its middle classes. Currently , over 50% of India population is under 25 years old by 2020 year . India will outpace China as the country with the largest tertiary age population.

Thus, Indian higher education is facing with four broad challenges, such as:

The supply –demand gap challenge: BY 2020 year, the Indian government aims to achieve 30% gross enrolment, which will mean providing to million university places, an increases of 14 million in six years.

The low quality of teaching and learning challenge: Shortage of faculty , poor quality teaching, outdated curricular, lack of accountability and quality assurance and separation of research and teaching.

Constraints on research and innovation challenge: With a very low level of PHD enrolment. India does not have enough high quality researchers, there are less opportunities for interdisciplinary and multidisciplinary working, lack or early stage research experience, a weak ecosystem for innovation and low levels of industry engagement.

Uneven growth and access to opportunity challenge: Socially access to higher education is uneven with inequalities in enrolment areas population groups and geographies.

Thus, India government needs to reform educational policy, but many predict higher education leader academics and policy makers in India to explore their views on what the future holds for them and link to collaborate with the UK. For example, India online educational organizations can co-operate with UK, USA etc. developed countries' famous and successful online educational institutes to apply internet to teach India students by distance learning method. If India students had any learning challenges , who can send their questions to enquire these overseas countries' lecturers to get feebacks easily by email channel. Also, India teachers can send email with overseas developed countries' teachers to discuss different teaching methods easily.

Thus, key challenges are facing the system includes online educational quality assurance, credit transfer system; between higher education and vocational skills solution method include promoting higher online education and vocational skills stream and online teacher training in higher education, change college education method to improve the quality of teaching and learning, private online educational business sector will continue to grow , but for profit high education is unlikely to be sanctioned soon international cooperating with UK institutions to make the most of educational opportunities and foreign education providers need to take a long term view and build closer multi -dimensional relationship with Indian institutions.

Consequently, online education will be the most suitable education method to solve India's many student increasing demand numbers when its school supply increasing number can not satisfy its student increasing demand number in India. Because India students do not need to go to schools, they can apply internet to learn at their home conveniently. It means that only online education can solve classrooms demand when India have many young students who need to go to school classrooms to learn. When they can apply internet to listen their teacher's teaching and they can enquire to their teacher from internet channel at home conveniently. Hence, online students' homes are similar to school's classrooms in India. India will be one online education development need country, due to its population is still increasing, but school numbers can not increase more than its student numbers.

2.2

● Course conent and learning and teaching factor influences online educational success.

I shall explain whether how to implement course content and learning and teaching method can raise teaching quality to online learning environment as below:

Interactive lecturing strategy
  ● Content and learning method

I shall recommend interactive lecturing strategies to raise online teaching quality. How to apply interactive lecturing strategies to raise participation in large group presentation? The use of interactive lecturers can promote active learning, high attention and motivation, give feedback to the teacher and the student, and increase techniques that can be used in large group presentations to achieve learning satisfaction for both.

For medical subject education example, interactive lecturing involves a two way interaction between the presenter and the participants (medical students). Interaction can also refer medical teaching material or the medical teaching content of a medical lecture. It does not necessary mean the talking. In all cases, however, interactive lecturing is implied active involvement and participation by the medical student (audience), so the medical students are no longer passive in the learning process. In giving this type of medical presentation, the medical " instructor" frequently becomes a " facilitator" or coach and more often than not, has to modify (change) the medical lecture content to allow for discussion and try new medical technique. Because medical students need to carry on medical practicing, so for any purpose of medical discussion and try new medical technique, refer to any large group medical presentation. It is important to note, however, that the number of medical students in the audience does not dictate whether the medical lecture can be interactive. Some way small medical student groups can be non-interactive, and certain interactive medical techniques can be incorporated into a class of over 200 medical students. Moreover, although large medical classes are most commonly considered the medical content for interactive lecturers, these medical techniques can also be used effective with smaller medical groups in the universities.

Why does university need an interactive lecture and how can it raise teaching quality? One of the major reasons for this critique is observation that lecturers are less effective than other methods when instructional goals involve the application of information or facts. However, when many teachers accept the notion that other teaching methods might be better than lecturers for encouraging students to be more actively involves in learning and for promoting the application of knowledge few have the time, resources or opportunity to use the small group methods to teach. Also, when done effectively, lecture can transmit new information in an efficient way, who can explain or clarify difficult notions, organize concepts and thinking, challenge beliefs, model problem solving and motive students to learn more easier from interacting lecturing. The value of interactive lecturing can let students have active participation and learning beyond the recall of facts and that students must be attentive and motivated in order for learning to occur. However, interactive lecturing can promote active involvement with the teaching can promote active material or the content, with the teacher or with classmate/peers.

Is teaching in class often simulated by questions or problem solving exercises as the students think about what who would answer in a particular situations? I feel these talking performance will increase attention and motivation to students and interactive lecturing strategy can encourage students to participate to ask questions in classroom. Because motivation is the essential ingredients for learning and often is more than intelligence to the student. I feel interactive lectures can simulate interest and help to maintain attention. By encouraging student to talk in classroom to be apply to feel life situations or focusing to use interactive lecturers in methods to motivate students read and learn more. How to evaluate interactive lecturing to facilities? In fact, interactive lecturing can facilitate these teaching material presented. It also assist teachers and students to solve problem and to assist to make decision, communication skills in classroom more easy. This is particularly important in medical education where the application of use of information is as important as recall of patient records of facts to carrying on researching. Moreover, interactive techniques allow teachers to receive feedback at a number of levels: on students needs (at the beginning, middle or end of a lecture), students on the other hand, can get feedback on their own knowledge or performance. In summary, participation on the part of the teacher interactive lecturing encourages active participation on the part of the teacher and the student. This method of teaching encourages student attention and allows for instant feedback on whether the lecture material has been understood.

How are commonly used from interactive techniques? These interactive teaching techniques have multiple benefits, so the instructor can easily and quickly assess of students have really mastered the studying materials and plan to dedicate move time to it, if necessary and the process of measuring student understanding in many cases is also practice for the study materials, often students don't actually learn the study material until of these assessments drives interactivity and brings several benefits. These interactive teaching techniques can let students feel more fun to listen a lecture to teach attentively in classroom.

The lecture instructor action includes, such as at the first, showing picture is as an image to students with no explanation, and asking them to identify or explain it and to justify their answers. Or asking students to write it using terms from lecture, or to name the processes and concepts down. Also, works are well as group activity. The lecturer can not give the answer to let students to know until who have explored all options first. At the second point, lecturer can ask a rhetorical question, and then allow 15-25 seconds, for students to think about the problem before the lecturers hope to wait to explain the question.

The technique encourages students to participate in the problem solving process, even when discussion isn't feasible to let students to write any questions and the lecturer also writes an answer or the same time. It aims to help assure that the students will work in fact on the problem. At the third point, the lecturer can ask a one word answer will suggest degree of comprehension. It aims to help students can learn to remember any new word easily. At the forth point, the instructors can illustrate a concept, idea or principle with a real life application model or cause study. The lecturer distribute a partially completed outline of today's lecture and ask student to fill it in. Useful at start or at end of class, which any student can write down personal opinion which concerns any controversial subject, then during finishing to teach any whole course in the end of the seminar. So the lecturer can gather all classroom opinion polls to aim to let the school to know what the students' feeling concern on the lecturer's teaching performance and the controversial subject content whether who feel more or less interest to learn their subject. Then, the school can evaluate whether it needs to change the subject's teaching contents or the lecturer's teaching method to satisfy whose further learning needs. At the fifth point, let students have chanced to perform whose feeling, e.g. students can either stand or sit to indicate whose answers, such as true or false to the instructor's questions, the lecturer can select some students to travel the classroom polling the others on a topic relevant to the course, then report back the results for everyone. At the sixth point, the lecturer can prepare a questionnaire for students that probes what kind of learning style who use, so the course can match visual learning styles. Also, the lecturer can provide a quote relevant to whose topic, but leave out a crucial word and ask students to guess what it might be. It aims to raise students interesting to learn the topic of contents. Then, the lecturer can ask the class to examine two written out version of a theory or law of nature concept etc. Where one is incorrect, such as the opposite or negation of the other. In deciding which is correct, students will have to examine the problem from all investigations. The lecturer design class activities or even essays to address the real lives of the individual students. Finally, the lecturer ought let student to perform these five steps: listen, stop, reflect, write, give feedback. So students can become self monitoring listeners Focused list several ideas related to the main focus point, helpful for starting new topics and using questionnaire (multi-choice or short answer). When introducing a new topic, assesses interest and preparation for the course, keeping track of the steps needed to solve specific types of problems. Model a list for students first and then asking them to perform similar steps.

Why do lecturers need to be trained to raise teaching quality? Nowadays, it is common that many small in scale, low in credibility and poorly supported educational institutions, are carrying on substantial training of 120 to 500 hours duration, is often compulsory and is sometimes linked to probation to lecturers. Increased confidence in the value of such training has not, however been based on solid evidence regarding the impact of training on teaching learning. Studies tend not to obtain evidence from theoretically or based questionnaires, obtain evidence from students or obtain evidence about impact on student learning to decide whether lecturers need to be trained. Education trainers are often articulate about what who are trying to achieve from their training methods and are finding whether who are trained successful. Education training is capable of achieving three of these goals: the improvement of teachers' skills; the development of teachers' conceptions of teaching and learning; consequent changes in students' learning. Other common goals of training, such as developing teachers' ability to reflect and be self-improving or to increasing self- confidence or self-efficiency , were not studied.

A teacher's approach to teaching has been shown to relate to the approach to study of their students, student-focused teachers are more likely to have students who take a deep approach (attempting to make sense of content) rather than a surface approach (attempting to remember content) (Trigwell et., 1999). However, much training is oriented towards developing teachers' teaching skills, especially whose classroom practice. Measures of teaching behavior have been shown to correlate with various measures of learning outcome. Some trainers need various measures of learning outcome. Some trainers are primarily oriented towards improving student learning, rather than towards improving teaching, and so their training is oriented towards changing teachers so that who are oriented towards student learning rather than towards teaching as performance.

One of the most notable trends in higher education branding and marketing is that institutions and dedicating more attention to hire marketing professionals from the corporate and have invested significant time and money to create strong institutional brands to build excellent teaching quality image. Perhaps the largest area of innovation and growth in higher education marketing and branding as well as in recruitment, is the online and digital space, some institutions polled use some form of social media as part of their marketing and overall operations to build excellent teaching quality image. Websities often feature elements, including narigation bars, engaging visuals, such as slidehows and prominent " call to actions" bottons that encourage students to apply for examples.

How can new technology influence to change teaching method to raise better teaching quality? Newer methods of online and technology enhanced course delivery, including flipped classrooms and instruction model in particular have resulted in greater student engagement. Adaptive learning technology has also enjoyed significant interest and new technologies are currently under development by Fujitsu, MIT and the Apolle Group.

As universities find the ever increasing and diverse student base, so successful branding can help with increasing enrollment, expanding fundraising capabilities and other outcomes, e.g. building excellent teaching quality image. Teaching technological method includes, responsive website design can be viewed on multiple devices and platforms; searching engine optimizaton, e.g. Google can be used to research new teaching programs particularly, colleages and universities can rely on data driven analytics to determine who, how, and where which are reaching audiences from web analytical software to gather students age, sex, choice, countries, client segments judge how to achieve teaching method strategies more easy from online technology.

It seems that the university would build better teaching quality image if it had better communication method with students. Because online communications can be committed to maintaining and improving teaching quality by gather facts data and evidence, such as rankings, accreditations, applicant data (number and quality), recruitment of professors, placement of graduates agreement with partners, media presence, anything that demonstrate the teaching quality, as the excellence of the institution helps and strengthens of its brand. It seems digital technology can assist any universities to build excellent teaching quality image more easily.

Can universities innovate its courses content to raise lecturers' teaching quality? For example, health and medicine, energy security and efficiency, education and defense and homeland security etc. high technologic subjects. Has it relationship between teaching quality and course content? I feel that attractive course content can influence individual lecturer to choose how to teach whose students to make them to raise enjoyable feeling more easily. So, research universities must need to improve management, productivity and cost efficiency in both administration and academics because young faculty have insufficient opportunities to launch academic courses and research programs. If universities hope students have more interesting to choose to study those subjects Doctoral and Postdoctoral preparation could be enhanced by shortenng time to degree, raising completion rated and enhancing programs' effectiveness in providing training for highly productive careers.

A recognition of the importance of supporting the comprehensive nature of the research university, academic and professional disciplines, including the physical, the arts and humanities courses innovation to enable universities to provide the research and education programs required by a knowledge and innovation-driven global economy. The nation's research universities should set and achieve goals in cost containment efficiency and productivity in business operations and academic programs innovation to attract students to have more courses interesting to choose to study those courses. Hence, internet learning and promotion methods can assist universities to reduce expenditures if which can build the excellent teaching quality image for long term. As, the traditional suppliers of higher education, universities today are operating in a rapidly changing environment. As well as coping with less resources, traditional learning (teaching) has evolved: access to information is now freely available online; with smart phones, mobile to learn. It changes the student individual habits and expectations. New online models represent a real opportunity to improve access to higher education. For example, demographic changes are opening up global opportunities for universities and new education producers. In Asia, many students need high quality education, such as China and India students have the need for new models for delivering education.

Limited public resources and information and knowledge now will freely available online, the old system of broad-based learning, institutional research and a large in house support staff is being shaken up. The market for online learning needs had been increasing every year. Asia's online degree programmes is growing at a rate of 17.3% faster than anywhere in the world. Seven out of the top 10 countries with the highest e-learning growth rates in the world are in Asia. It seems Asia will be the popular new online education market. Moreover, many universities are also starting to offer more model of learning, students are taught using a mixture of online learning and face-to-face fuition rather than solely through traditional lecturing. It seems online and face-to-face education method will have chance to raise teaching quality among either only face-to-face classroom or only online education method. So it seems that teaching method can influence teaching quality. We can't rely on delivering content anywhere, it is all about contextualisation ways of thinking and the student experience. Traditionally, universities hold key to knowledge in both a physical and philosophical sense. University libraries faculty and research institutes were where knowledge was created, stored and shared. Now, students hope to absorb knowledge with a device and connectivity, not just facts and figures, but also analysis and interpretation.

Today, access is expanding both in developed markets, such as Australia and even more fundamentally in China's tertitary education market. As China education participation rate had raised from 8% to 25.9% in the first decade of this century, and is likely to double again in the next 10 to 15 years. For universities, this will drive new approaches to teaching and learning create opportunities for entry to new innovating education markets and new low cost distribution in area, for quality of education needs. For example, digital technologies won't cause the disappearance of the campus-based university. Campuses will exist as places of teaching and learning, research, community engagement and raised forms of student experience. Assuming universities can deliver a rich, on campus experience. But, digital technology will transform the way education is delivered and supported, for example, through applications that enable real time student feedback, the way education is accessed in remote and regional areas, both in the developed and developing world.

Online teaching can provide attrative image to let science students to raise learning more interesting. How does learning about scientists during their scientific knowledge building affect students' science learning? For example, a control group in which students mainy learned information about the physic contents, who were studying how to increase students' interest in physical lessons, recall of science concepts, and physical problem solving. How can lecturer help scientific subject students create perceptions of scientists at hardworking individuals to make scientific progress? In addition, it also increased their delayed recall of the key science concepts and improved their abilities to solve complex problems. So, any lecturer needs to provide an opportunity for students to relate scientists to their knowledge-building activities has important implications for science learning and instruction. How does lecturer increase efforts to students' motivation to learn by creating instructional materials , e.g. textbooks or computer-based instructional materials that are more interesting, fun, or engaging for students ? For instance, many science text-books incorporate stimulating illustrations or visual images are in order to motivate students to learn the context. Another common approach to increase motivation is to promote students' interest in science by enhancing the overall reability of the texts. The efforts are undoubtedly important for science education as textbooks.

● Online Classroom management knowledge method

How to set goal to motivate and to educate science subject students more easily from online learning channel? Some education professionals (educators) had encouraged how to use effort belief to motivate students' learning, particularly in the area of science education is to use stories that illustrate scientists' stuggles toward new discoveries. Many science educators have suggested that a scientist's personal narratives, anecdote, self-reflections or life stories are valuable resources to inspire science learning (Eshach, 2009; Haven, 2007;Klopter, 199; Martin & Brouwer, 1991, 1993; McKinney & Michalovic, 2004; Milne, 1998; Rowcliffe, 2004; Solomon, 2002; Stinner, 1995; Stinner & Williams, 1993). So, it seems that any educator ought depend on the subject's unique feature or characteristics to decide how to teach whose students. So, teaching science subject, the educator needs to give himself/herself life story, self reflections in order to raise the subject's attraction and whose students' interesting to learn the science subject. Because a scientist's intellectual, personal and social struggles that led to important inventions and discoveries, if the educator can give personal life experience to let students to feel how who can encounter science to whose daily life. Then, it is possibe that the educator's personal life experience can lead whose students to create important inventions and discoveries during who will become scientists in the future.

In special, the science educators also need to design of an online learning environment to provide to whose students to explore science at their own pace and in their spare time. Therefore, all of the self study activities took place in an online learning environment. One main reason for this design was high speed internet access, but lacked meaningful online learning resources. The informal online learning environment was designed to serve as a resource to supplement the school's formal science instruction. Also the online lessons consisted of the following two components: the first is science content, consisting of the physical lessons described above, and the second is achievement oriented stories about the scientists, including the image of the scientists and their personal backgrounds. It aims to raise students' interest in science research.

Why do higher education need to raise teaching quality? For India higher education needs example, India has a low rate of the supply and demand enrolment gap nowadays, at only 18%, compared with 26% in China and 36% in Brazil. There is unmet demand for higher education. The reason is the low quality of teaching and learning is providing to India's higher education system. The system is beset by issues of quality in many of its institutions, a shortage of faculty, poor quality teaching, outdated and lack of accountability and quality assurance and separation of research and teaching. With a very low level of PHD enrolment, India doesn't have enough high quality researchers, there are few opportunities for interdisciplinary and multidisciplinary workng, lack of early stage research experience, a weak ecosystem for innovation and low levels of education industry engagement in India education system. So, India education institutions are facing challenges to influence the low enrolment rate. Although, India's population is growing, but it's higher education student numbers is decreasing. I believe the factor causing is main source from the poor lacking quality. Hence, India educators need to spend more time to research how to improve their educational methods to attract many students to enrol to universities to study.

Goal setting is one important factor to influence the country's education system or the school's teaching method succeed whether it can success or fail to improve its teaching quality. Goal setting is the process of estabishing an outcome (a goal) to serve as the aim of one's actions. In educational settings, the ultimate outcome is usually some form of learning as operationalized by the instructor and/or the students (Marzano, Pickering, & Pollock, 2001, p.93).

Setting goals can be specially important for students with low achievement motivation. In an experimental study, authors identified college students as having either high or low achievement motivation. Students in each group, were then randomly placed into either goal setting group where they decided how may anagram who would solve or into the control groups (Horn & Murphy, 1985). The research result indicated that when students with high achievement motivation performed equally well in both goal conditions, self-set goals enhanced the performances of students with low achievement, motivation. Therefore, instructors may encourage students to set goals if whose motivation to achieve is low.

How schools can set goals and what schools make a good goal to which student. The most important step toward goal attainment is to set effective goals. There are many factors that influence the effectiveness. Studies have documented that individuals with clear, written goals are significantly more likely to succeed. Then, whose without clearly defined goals. In a study conducted by Ferguson and Sheldon (2010), participants write " why and how" who will achieve a goal. There was an interaction between the level of initial goal-relevant skills and the effectiveness of writing "why or how" of the goals. Students with initially low goal-relevant skills were more likely to internalize their goals over time and report greater goal expectancies of who wrote about the "how" of the goals. Therefore, education ought not neglect to encourage whose students to attract to write what whose goals are and explain why there are their goals and how to plan to achieve their goals. It aims to build their confidence to know why who choose to study the subject and how who need to study the subject to achieve their study plan successfully. So, procedural written goals are strategies that students may use to achieve a goal, such as learning a problem solving strategy. For example,outcomes goals strategies are specific to an activity at hand, such a solving fraction problems or writing an essay on specific procedure and outcome goals on students' motivation, learning and self-efficacy. Suchunk and Rice (1991) found that the best way to promote self-efficacy and achievement is to couple the process goal with progress feedback on now well the students use a strategy.

Why educators need to encourage students to set whose goals to learn in their learning process. Because students need to know their progress toward their goals, especially when working an accomplishing procedure goals. Also instructors can give feedback that stresses processes, such as how well student are using a strategy, budgeting their time, and completing subgoals. When instructors implement outcome goals, who may consider giving students feedback on how well who are doing currently compared with low who did previously. Such comparisons would raise student self-efficacy, ultimately, student should learn to monitor their goals and analyze the progress made toward attaining them. So, written setting goals is a learning progress to let students to write to remember what whose goals planning are and to remember why these are whose goals and to remember how who plan to achieve whose goals in their learning process. If who forget what are whose goals or subgoals and /or how to achieve their goals or subgoals and/or why these are their goals or subgoals in their learning process any time. Then, who can take their written note to remember again and to revise whether who can improve their ability to achieve their goals or subgoals in any stage during their learning process. Till to the end of the course, who can revise what the factors are caused to their failure to get poor grade and how to avoid solve the challenges will be caused in next time learning process. Hence, goal setting is a good educational psychological method to prepare to choose the best educational method and course content and to build/raise students' confidence to learn more easily during whose learning process in schools. I suggest educators ought use this education method to let whose students to attempt to practise in any course beginning.

● online teaching technique

I think content knowledge can be a barrier to any online teacher individual teaching skillful development. The problem is when the eductional content becomes the be-all and end-all of the teaching process. When the content matters more than anything. When course content is that important, faculty are prevented from using methods that enhance how much students learn. In this case, the educational course content orientation of faculty hurts students and teachers in possible.

When teachers think the only, the best, the most important way to improve their teaching is by developing their content knowledge, who neglect to consider the teaching contents levels of knowledge, but who have only simplistic instructional methods to convey that teaching material. Both are essential what teachers teach and how who teach it are linked and very much dependent on one another.

Even though both are tightly linked, which are still separate. Development of one doesn't automatically improve how the other functions. So teachers can work to grow teaching content knowledge, but if the methods used to convey that knowledge are not sophisticated, teaching may still be quite ineffective. It may not motivate students efficient, as well as it may not result in more and better student learning. Because teachers only feel whose teaching content most the best educational quality.

The typical college teacher has spent years in courses developing the knowledge still set and virtually no time on the teaching set. This way of preparing professors assumes that the content is much more complex than the process, when in fact both are not equally fair to treat. The teaching content and the process requires the best knowledge level to be prepared to teachers to teach. Some kinds of contents are the best taught by example, some by experience. Other kinds are the best understood when discussed and worked on colloboratively other kinds need individual reflection and analysis. Besides these learning and teaching both demands of the content itself, there are the learning needs of individual student.

The best teachers are not always, no even usually, those teachers with the most sophisticated content knowledge. The best teachers ought know their teaching material, but who also ought know a lot about the teaching process. They follow themselves instructional methods, teaching strategies and approaches, just as whose content knowledge develops. They never underestimate the power of the teaching process to determine the outcome. With this understanding, content is not a barrier to teacher development.

How to identify effective teaching methods for the large class environment? What teaching methods are effective in the large class environment? What are students' perceptions of these methods? In common, used teaching methods include lecture, discussion, combination, case study, team project which were applied and evaluated in a large class setting. In addition, improvement on student feelings about large versus small classes and student opinions of the teaching methods was gathered.

Large class environment is needed to offer strategies for course design, student engagement, active learning and assessment. The advantage of large classes include decreased instructor costs, efficienct use of faculty time and talent , availability of resources and standardization of the learning experence. But, there are significant disadvantages to large class teaching environment including impersonal relations between students and the instructor, limited range of teaching methods, discomfort among instructors teaching large classes.

Has it relationship between class size and student performance to influence teaching quality. The traditional passive view of learning involves situations where material is delivered to students using a lecture based format. In contrast, a more modern view of learning is constructivism, where students are expected to be active in the learning process by participating in discussion and/or collaborative activities (Fosnot, 1989). Some educational professionals suggested that lecture leaded to the ability to recall facts, but discussion produced higher level comprehension. Further, research on group-oriented discussion methods had shown that team learning and student-led discussions didn't only produced favorable student performance outcomes, but also raised greater student participation in large class. In terms of students' preferences for teaching methods, a study by Qualters (2001) suggests that "students do not favor active learning methods because of the in-class time taken by the activities, fear of not covering all of the material in the course, and anxiety about changing from traditional classroom expectatons to the active structure". I suggest that lecturers can assess of the course, perferences for class size to decide perceptions of teaching methods. Students were asked a series of questions to gather information on their perceptions of the course, as well as their prefeences for class size 89% of respondnts indicated that the course has been of value to them, likewise 90% of respondents indicated that who had learned a lot in the course and 86% rated. The topic material is interesting. 51% of respondents indicated a preference for small class sizes less than 50 students .

Effective management of large classes is a popular topic among faculty in higher education, it is possible that universities feel which will influence lecturers' teaching quality to satisfy student's individual learning needs. However, some surveys indicated that 99% of respondents reported that who were currently enrolled in large classes generally. However, the surveys' result could conclude that these teaching methods were accepted positively to affect student's individual learning needs. Students scores improved most under the jigsaw method, and least under the team project method, whereas the lecture, lecture/discussions and case study methods produced similar improvement. The finding suggested that moderately active learning methods, such as the jigsaw method is more effective than the lecture, lecture/discussions and case study method. However, more extreme active learning methods, such as team projects completed outside of class may not be as effective as moderately -active or passive teaching method.

The findings of the study also demonstrate that most students (51%) have a preference for small class sizes (less than 50 students). However, some students (38%) indicated no preference for class size,when the remaining 10% indicated a preferene for large classes 100 or more large classes. So, it implied that most students did not like large class environment to study. However, the finding indicated the lecture/discussion teaching method was the most preferred among students. Students commented as to their reason for selecting this as the most valuable method who have a desire to be an action learners engaging in discussion rather than passively listening to a lecture.

Can measure teacher effectiveness to judge whether the teacher individual teaching quality is achieved to the minimum requirement? Generally, on Asia countries, teachers need even more sophisticted abilities to teach more complex educational resources at home, who are new english language learners, and those who have distinctive learning needs.

In recent years, there has been growing interest in moving beyond traditional measures of teacher qualifications, such as completion of a preparation program, number of degees, or years of experience, in order to evaluate teachers' actual performance as the basic for making decision about hiring. How should we measures teacher efectiveness? So, how to judge whether the teaching quality is achieved to the minimum requirement, for nursing engineering, accounting, medicine and other skilled professions etc. subjects.

Why do teachers need performance assessment to raise teaching quality? How well teachers have developed the classroom teaching skills to be effective with their students, a graduate's commitment to teaching as a professional career, feedback from graduates and employers and high quality tests of their knowledge and skills that are tied to classroom teaching performance. I believe that new assessments are needs to tell whether teacher education graduated have developed the classroom teaching skills to be effective with their students because current teacher tests don't directly measure what teachers do in the classroom, and who don't indicate how well teachers will do in the classroom.

In nearly all states, teachers have to pass at least three tests, generally multiple choice tests of basic skills, subject matter and teaching knowledge, in order to become licensed, even though these are not strongly related to their ultimate success in the classroom. Furthermore, in many cases these tests evaluate teacher knowledge before who enter or complete teacher education, and hence are an inadequate tool for teacher education accountability.

Performance assessment aims to measure what teachers actually do in the classroom, and which have been to be related to later teacher effectiveness. So, this method has potential to raise teaching quality in possible. It can be a value added method for examining student learning gains into teacher evaluation. As Harvard University economics professor Thomas Kane pointed out in recent senate testimony, these measures have been subject to concerns about their ability at the individual teacher level and the possibility who could teach toward narrow tests, as well as the fact, who are not available for about three-fourths of all teachers. So, whose obsevational measures is due to the fact that the sore gains measure more than the influence of the teacher, even when statistical methods are used to control for other factors, such as student characteristics, home and school resources and the influence of other teachers, tutors, and parents on learning. Furthermore, also most expects agree that at least three years of data about a given teacher are necessary to achieve a stability, the direct use of student test score data to evaluate teachers doesn't help inform judgements about new entrants to the education profession.

However, I commend that how certain kinds of classroom observations and videotapes of teaching, teacher reflectations, context pedagogical assessments and student and teacher feedback can be related to measures of teacher effectiveness, based on student achievement gains on both traditional tests and more intellectually challenging open-ended measures. These methods can raise teaching quality indirectly. Thus, effort to create more consistency in evaluating teacher performance are critical if performance is to be a central measure of teacher effectiveness.

● Meauring student studying method

What is online teacher and online student learning motivation relationship on online students' individual online classroom learning environment ? I believe that the quality of student's relationships with teacher and peer is a fundamental substrate for the development of academic engagement and achievement and it can influence teaching quality. It is easy to think students are learning forward in their seats, hands waving, questions and opinions rolls out, offering the teacher a clear picture of what students understand and where confusion remains. Students like to attempt groups learning and continue discussions, showing their comprehension through questions, critical listening and arguing about examples, who apply the material to whose own lives . The teacher is thoroughly energized, thinking about how the material to be covered next builds on that day's class.

Student engagement and motivation are precious commodities, valuable not only to teachers but also to students. Students school lives are more enjoyable when who are engaged in their classes. I think student intrinsic motivation is a factor which can influence whose learning ability from the teacher's teaching . So the teacher's teaching behavior is a extrinsic motivation to excite whose students to feel whose teaching quality level is high or low (satisfactory or non satisfactory). The caring teacher and student relatinships and high quality peer relationships for student academic self-perceptions, school engagement, motivation, learning and teaching performance, which does close influence. Teachers and students recognize high quality relationships , who seem effortless because who are intrinsically motivating, enjoyable and mutually reinforcing. Teachers and students also know when relationships are not working, and unfortunately, such relationships are also self-sustaining in ways that detract frm instruction and erode classroom cohesion. To support teachers in meeting this challenge.

I shall attempt to explain why classroom relationships work and don't work and to offer practical strategies to help teachers to improve the motivational dynamics of difficult relationships. The bottom line is that teachers are forced to spend more time engaged in activities who feel compete with good teaching. It is easy to imagine high quality relationships in the classroom. Interactions are courteous and kind, and who focus on learning them material and building academic skills ; students provide constructive criticism and are receptive to feedback, the classroom is welcoming but focused on academics.

Why do these relationships work? An useful way of explaining the complex dynamics of relationships is through the motivational model. To raise teaching quality to let students to feel teachers need provide structured interactions in which teaches need set high standards, clear expectations and reasonable limits for students' behaviors and performance and consistently follow through on their demands. Optimal structure includes teachers' confidence in students' abilities as well as help students figure out how to reach high levels of understanding and performance.

Finally, teachers' autonomy support shapes student motivation , when teachers treat students with respect and seek out, listen to and value their opinions. Therefore, it has good relationship between the teacher and whose students. Then, students feel who are considered and feel the teacher can provide good educational (teaching) quality as the same time . So, every teacher needs consideration to student's engagement of emotion.

Why has it close relationship between raising teaching quality and the teacher is effective ? There is only one way to obtain student achievement and the research is very specific. It is the teacher and what the teacher knows and can do that is the determining factor with student achievement. Any students will learn based on whether the teacher is effective or ineffective. I feel that district variables don't matter; school variables don't matter; program variables don't matter; It is the teacher that matter. Because the ineffective teachers get poor results. Otherwise, the effective teachers get good results and it makes no difference to the good teacher. What teachers give whose students. What programs who teach them and who the administrators are. The bottom line is that there is one way to create good schools, without good teachers as well as it is the administrator who creates a good school and it is the teacher who creates a good school and it is the teacher who creates a good classroom.

Is shortage of good teaching discipline relationship not provide good quality of teaching ? It is really quite simple to solve this challenge. Institutions can fix leak by providing adequate training and support for beginning teachers (known as indication), thereby, increasing the retention of more competent, qualified and satisfied professionals for classrooms. Due to the reason, teacher is the only factor that can improve student achievement. The major problem of lack of procedures and routines and discipline can influence the quality of teaching. So, if the school had good classroom management skills, then it can substantially improve student achievement. Therefore, effective classroom management skill can cause effective teaching, then effective teaching can raise good quality of teaching to let students to enjoy learning benefits form the teachers.

I shall indicate these three questions: What is quality teaching and why it is important in higher education? How can teaching concretely be enhanced? How can one make sure quality teaching initiatives are effective?

Nowadays, quality teaching has become an issue of important changing, increased interactive competition, increasing social and geographical diversity of the student body, increasing demands of value for money, introduction of information techniques etc. Quality teaching initiatives are very diverse both in nature and in function. However, research points out that quality teaching is necessarily student-centred. It's aim is most and all student learning. Thus, attention should be given simply to the teacher's opinion of teaching.

Quality teaching has become an issues of importance to higher education. The student body has consideraby expanded and diversified, both socially and geographically. New students call for new teaching methods. Modern technologies have entered the classroom, thus modifying the nature of the interactions between students and professors. The governments, the students and their families, the employers, the fund providers increasingly demand value for their money and desire more efficiency through teaching. In fact, conceptions of quality teaching happen to be stakeholder relative : students, teachers or evaluation agencies don't share the definition what good teaching or good teacher is. In general, good teachers have empathy for students, who are generally experienced teachers and most of all who are generaly experienced teachers and most of all who are organized and expensive, those who have passions: passions for learnings for their field, for teaching and for their students. But research also demonstrates that good teaching depends on what is being taught and on other situational factor. Some research -centred, it's aim is most and for all student learning.

Thus, attention should be given not simply to the teacher's teaching skills, but also to the learning environment that must address the student's personal needs: students should know why who are working, should be also to relate to other students and to receive help if needed. Adequate support to staff and students (financial support, social and academic support, support to minority students, conseling services etc.), also improves learning outcomes. So, groups of students and/or teachers who need learn and build knowledge through intellectual interaction, are judged to enhance on student learning by inceasing students' and teachers' satisfaction.

How can teaching be enhanced to raise quality? Quality teaching initiatives are very diverse both in nature and in function. The most currently used quality initiatives seem to aim to enhance teamwork between teachers, goal-setting and course plans. However, gathering information and reading the literature, are looking outside the classrooms, are important fools to improve quality of teaching, but who are still under-employed. Another point to keep in mind, how to enhance student learning. The focus of quality teaching initiatives should not always be on the teacher. Rather it should encompass the whole institution and the learning environment. Another of major drivers for enhancemnt of quality teaching concerns teachers' leadership. However the role of the department, of the educational support divisions and that of the central university, which can value quality culture part of its mission statement are central.

How can school make sure quality teaching is effective? I recommend that it is essential to measure the impact of the quality teaching initiatives in order to be able to improve these initiatives. However, assessing the quality of one's teaching remains challenging. The choice of indicators to measure quality teaching is important, because it has been shown that assessment drive-learning, how the teacher is judged with undoubtedly impact whose teaching methods. Indicators to access the quality of teaching (the value of graduates, satisfaction of teachers, retention rates etc.) of an institution proved of case but carry various meanings and even lead to misunderstandings. Researchers agree that reliable indicators should be chosen, and not just the most practical ones. Moreover, classroom management skills should be discussed for teacher's individual method how to influence quality of teaching.

Assessing the results of quality teacing initiatives has proven to be difficult, and this issue has received increasing attention in the literature. What are the experiences, purposes and methods to support quality teaching? What are the major drivers that support quality teaching and the factors that hinder quality teaching? How traditional and innovative methods are used to assess and improve quality teaching initiatives? In fact, the difficulties may teachers in higher education are encountered with when assessing the impact of those initiatives that are meant to enhance the quality of teaching. The fact that a great proportion of studies on quality teaching were carried out on a very limited scale (specifically concerned with a small group of students or specific disciplines of study).

What is quality teaching and why is it important in higher education? How can teaching be enhanced? How can one make sure quality teaching initiative are effective? I shall force on teaching inputs and learning outcomes. Instead of focusing simply on the question of what a good teacher is, I feel that a good or excellent tacher may indeed help whose students, but whose contribution to the field of teaching will be weak if who does not share whose discoveries with whose colleagues or analyze whose own methods. Also I believe the quality of learning environment can be improved if teaching should be both research-formed and research driven.

Nowadays, students are therefore very concerned about the quality of the lecturers who pay for. Next, the internet has globalised the market place, and the institutions are increasingly competing for the best students, nationally international students, and consequently may develop now teaching strategies. Teaching methods concern aspects of online learning need to become familiar with new teaching methods. Distance education in print form is being supplemented by internet, based delivery. Mixed modes of learning have become common: the majority of cross border distance programmes now involves some form of face-to-face or administrator contact, sometimes visits to study centres. Generally people in remote locations and working adults are the student role to attempt this new form of learning. As globalization continues, the international competiton for the best students is likely to increase among higher education institutions, thus among reinforcing pressure for quality teaching. It is likely that international rankings based on the quality of teaching will be attractive of quality initiatives.

Harvey and Green (1993) distinguisg four definitions of quality that can help us to understand what quality teaching might be. First, quality is as excellence, the traditional conception of quality is the dominant one. Second, quality can be defined as value for money, a quality institution in this is one that satisfies the demands of public accountability. Third, quality may seen as fitness for purpose, the purpose being that of the students to learn sciences efficiently. The last, definition explained quality as transforming, it means quality teaching is teaching that transforms students' perceptions and the way who go about applying their knowledge to real world problems . Quality assurance in higher education has also become a focus of attention for private universities. Students who are increasingly paying tuition fee might now be considered as clients of higher education institutions. It caused that students are also my concerned about the quality of lectures who pay for. As the culture of higher education has become increasingly market-oriented and external demands for quality of teaching have increased.

Teaching methods have also changed. Professors who wish to use online education method to teach students. Because of all these changes, several questins has been caused: can the possessive of a PHD be taken as a proxy for teaching competence? What constitutes good and approriate teaching? How can a quality culture in higher education, that supports quality teaching be defined and achieved? Dickinson et al. (1995) point out that " education may be unique in the sense that it is difficult for the client to assess the quality and relevance of the service (p.63).

In fact, it sometimes happens that only years after an university course, a student at least comes to understand why this particular courses was useful. Another side, some educators identified quality culture was based on two distinct elements: a set of value, belief, expectations and commitment towards quality, a structural/ managerial element with well defined processes that enhance quality and coordinate effects. However, it has relationship between quality teaching and quality culture relationship. Because every classroom has different learning culture, learning environment, teaching performance, teaching resources, educational time spending, learning of satisfaction level. So, educators need to understand whose classroom and students culture, then, who may have more ability to understand how to teach whose students in the classroom more easily.

The role and status accorded to teachers is being reassessed increase. Indeed, it is easy to understand that the quality of its teachers. But in order to enhance and reward teaching excellence, it is essential to know what constitutes good teaching. Good teaching depends on whom and what is being taught. It concerns between student entry characteristics and effective teaching behaviors. In general, content-unfamiliar students' perception of learning is more positively influenced by the professor's organization than by the professor's expressiveness. However, students who are familiar with the course content are more sensitive to the professor's expressiveness than to whose organization skill.

In conclusion, student individual learning emotion and educational environment and teacher individual teaching method and classroom management and their relationship and learning and teaching culture these factors can influence overall quality of teaching to any higher education institutions.

2.2 Developing countries traditional classroom learning challenges

Future challenges influence high education development in long term

Nowadays, developing countries, such as India, China, Korea, Thailand, Hong Kong etc. are facing educational challenges. I feel developing countries governments have responsibilities to consider every citizens who can have effort to study or learn in themselves countries fairly. How to achieve the politician education is seen as a solution to poverty , social mobility, equality of opportunity, social problems, management of the changes in values educational systems, the key productivity and human resource development in primary, secondary and tertiary different student learning stages of educational aspects.

To the developing countries teachers, education is seen as that which should contribute to the development of the potential of the child to contribute to the development of the nation and by extension " world development". The development countries can't provide excellent education quality and quantity to students . They have these similar characteristics to influence to develop their education : relatively small population , small land area, limited natural resources, range of diversity , high level of dependency on international forces, economic challenges. Thus, I feel they need education reform, the perceptions of the important of education and the limitations are faced by both terms of quality and quantity has resulted on reduction reform. Education reform means the implication of globalization methods . It necessary to reform their education systems for it requires them to adapt their own education content to meet not only their local demands, but also their international concerns.

These developing countries educational major challenges, include these aspects mainly: on economic aspect, under educational level youth unemployment, skill shortages in key areas of the economy, new jobs associated with higher technology occupations requiring higher entry levels, a mismatch between the graduates and the available jobs. On social aspect, the non-educational students spend waste time to do bad behaviors to influence whose relationships between families or teachers in societies. Doing bad behaviors , such as illegal international drug trade, high crime rate and gang warfare, HIV/AIDS disease increasingly the case of death rate for those between the age of 15 and 45 years the largest crime age group.

Thus, developing country governments need how to solve these challenges. On changing environment aspect, it concerns on the nature and organization of work, the need for retraining and retooling , the important role of knowledge or a factor of production, the emphasis on information technology. On political aspect, it concerns on a democracy, peace, a creation of a state of esteem society.

In general, these development have these major challenges on education aspect: Existing curriculum content and pedagogical methods are being questioned. Students leave school ill-prepared for the world of work and adulthood, high incidence of illiteracy and numeracy, marked gender differences in achievement, curriculum changes without the necessary changes in assessment, untrained teachers at the early childhood, primary and secondary levels. Student under-performance , high levels of student attrition, student repetition of grade levels, harmonization of curriculum and assessment across the region , inadequate policy for recruitment and selection of teachers, lack of systems of certification evaluation and licensing of teachers, unsure about eh place of tech/voc. In secondary schools, the harmonization of competencies, skills for certification of students for the world of work.

To conclude, any developing countries major educational challenges have these characteristics: there seems to be no other alternative right now and in the near future for them, but to collaborate in all areas of development utilizing the new technologies and benefiting from those that have begun the change process at the same time, maximizing the resources at their immediate disposal.

The question demonstrates how universities have responded the pressures created by the country's economic recession. For example, universities in the UK are already being seriously affected by the short term impact of both economic recession and the crisis in public finances.

The more substantial reductions in expenditure now awaited are likely to increase the existing planned cuts to create major existing challenges to which the sector must respond. The UK economic recession and the public funding crisis are closely related, but which are not the same. However, UK universities have been facing some short term challenges, such as changes in student choices and graduate employment, due to consequences of economic recession in UK. Because it can influence UK students feel lack confidence about how the subjects that students wish to study and the kind of employment who find on leaving higher education in the future. Thus, it has close relationship between the UK economy changes in the post-recession world, as well as with the changes in student support and graduate contribution.

How other governments and other higher education systems have responded to economic recession in the short term. I suggest governments need to concern why economic recession had caused , it is as part of a long term strategy to build intellectual capital (knowledge economy). Increasing investment in higher education significant increases in funding for research, a stabilization of the per capita teaching grant and the introduction of higher and deferred fees for undergraduates. Engaging with business in knowledge transfer, skills and internships to universities to promote what subject(s) will be the most popular and successful teaching subject(s) in the univeristy and explaining the reasons why these subjects can attract students to study from internet knowledge exchange channel. These internet teaching promoting method will be possible to solve economic challenges to influence global students to make university choice to study more easily.

Future challenges India and China medical education

China and India is the most populated geographical area of the world (1.2 billion in India). Thus, medical service will be much demanded in India. However, China and India have the largest number of medical challenges, but they can't provide excellent quality health care to patients. Why such a situation has arisen in India and China? The problem is the clinical settings where doctors avail training.

In recent years, technology and health care systems have profound changes. To cope with these changes , medical educational institutions around the world have been increasingly confronted with the challenge of making their curricula more meaningful and relevant to the needs of the community. So, apply technology method to learn medical education and suggested strategies for direction is needed to adopt the medical education changes.

For example, many medical schools have now translated into all major languages, has been very widely adopted as basis for reform of medical education. So, India and China medical lecturers can teach their mother language to compare English teaching to let medical students to understand what their teaching more easily. Many of the medical schools in Asia have traditional teacher –centered and hospital based training with a few exceptions only. Medical teachers , planners and policy makers are to be well-informed of such trends and utilize these in planning, implementing and evaluating medical training programs to increase relevance and quality and to produce need-based human resources for health for the regions, such as India and China. So, internet will be the best language learning method for these medical lecturers and students.

What medical problem to Indian and Chinese face? Indian and Chinese get a significant number of medical tourists, a reflection of the high level of medical expertize that Indian and Chinese patients possess . However, a majority of India and China citizens have limited assess to quality health care, less than half of Indian and Chinese children are fully immunized. Similarly, the minimum of three checkups during pregnancy remains unavailable for half of Indian and Chinese pregnant women. India and China universities are just degree selling shops. Medical schools should make changes in the curriculum, adopt innovate strategies for enhancing students' learning improve the methods used to assess students' performance and focus on the professional development of faculty as teachers and educators.

In China and India , medical students follow a rote method of learning, so the clinical bedside knowledge is far below the requirement . How is this going to make India and China reliable doctors? In conclusion, medical education is a professional subject. So, China and India need concern how well to train doctors' skills to prepare to provide excellent medical service to their patients to achieve health satisfactory level to every hospitals. Online/distance learning learning channel will be one good method to let medical students to learn when they live so far distance to their university in India or China.

Reference

ACT 2006. Developing the STEM education pipleing
IOWA city IA: ACT.

American Association Of State College And Universities, 2005. " Strengthening the science and math. pipeline for a better American policy matters vol. 2, number 11 . Nov. /Dec.

Critical thinking rubric created by the Catalina Foothills School District, http://rubrics.metiri, wikispaces.net/file/view/ Calalina_Foothills_Critical_Thinking_Rubric_1.doc

Digest Of Education Statistics 1020. Retrieved from http://nces.edu.gov/pubsearch/pubsinfo.asp?pubid=2011015

OCED program for international assessments (PISA) 2009 results. Retrieved from http:// www.oecd. org/edu/pisa/2009.

Nagel, D. " Cloud computer to make up 35% of k-12 budgets in 4 years." IT trends research, The Journal February 19, 2013. http://the journals.com/articles/201302/19/cloud-computing-to-make-up-35-of-k12-it-budgets

Zinth, Kyle, 2006 Recent State STEM Initiatives.
Denver: Education Commission to the states.

Reference

Dickinson, K.D. Pollock, A, & Troy, J. (1995), " perceptions of the value of quality assessment in scottis higher education", Assessment and evaluation in higher education, vol. 20, no 1, pp. 59-66.

Eshach, H. (2009). The Nobel Prize In The Physics Class: Science, history and glamour. Science & Education, 18, 1377-1393. doi: 10.1007/s
11191-008-9172-4.

Ferguson, Y., & Sheldon, K.M. (2010). Should goal
strivers, think about "why " or "how" to strive?
It depends on their skill level. Motivation and
emotion 34-253-265.

Fosnot, C. (1989). Enquiring teachers, enquiring learners. New York: Teachers college press.

Harvey, L. & Green, D. (1993) " Defining quality",
Assessment and evaluation in higher education,
vol, 18, pp.8-35.

Horn, H.L. & Murphy, M.D. (1985). Low need achievers' performance: The positive impact of
a self-determined goal. Personality and social
psychology Bulletin, 11, 275-285.

Marzano, R.J., Pickering, D.J., & Pollock, J.E. (2001). Classroom instruction that works.
Alexandria, VA: ASCD.

Qualters, D. (2001). Do students want to be active?
The Journal of job.

Schunk, D.H., & Rice, J.M. (1991). Learning goals and progress feedback instruction. Journal of reading behavior. 23, 351-364.

Trigwell, K., Prosser, M. & Waterhouse, F. (1999)
Relations Between Teachers' Approaches To
Teaching And Students' Approaches To
LearningHigher Education 37: 57-70.

THREE

THE GROWTH RATE OF ONLINE LEARNING GRADUATED STUDENT NUMBER IMPROVES THE TRADITIONAL CLASSROOM LEARNING METHOD

Firstly, I suppose it has relationship between online education and the graduate student increasing number to any developed or developing countries both nowadays. Such as online teacher human capital and online education factor, such as online course or subject design factor, online teacher individual teaching skill and online teacher teaching experience factor which have close relationship to influence every online student individual learning ability to pass every online subject more easily.

Hence, the online students will feel less difficulties in order to pass every online subject to achieve graduate easily. Hence, in long term, it is possible that online graduated student number will increase more fast more than the traditional classroom learning graduate student number in long term. However, some economists indicate the evidence on the relationship between online teacher human capital and online graduated student number growth and who conclude that there is strong evidence that online teacher individual teaching skill and online teaching experience of human capital can raise the online student individual ability to pass every online subject more easily. Suggesting that online education really is online learning productivity-enhancing, rather than traditional classroom education is used by individuals to signal their ability to potential employers.

The primary measures are used to capture the average level of online teacher human capital per online teaching worker include:

I. The average number of years of online teaching schooling of the online skillful teacher workforce or population, which assumes a linear relationship with online teaching human capital.

II. The share of the online skillful teacher workforce population with specific educational qualifications.

III. Online school enrolment rates, specially as a starting value. This flow into online education is often used as stock of online teaching qualifications and is available for developed Asia countries, e.g. Hong Kong, Japan and developing Asia countries, e.g. China, Korea both.

However, developing Asia countries have potential problems arising from measurement errors in online education, as the average schooling levels are derived from enrolment flows. They adopt more reliable country online education level micro data and find a positive result or response between the online graduated student number growth rate of online education. Online teacher supply (Human capital) flows are most commonly provided by online school enrolment rates, have been widely used in studies of the relationship between online teacher human captial and the online graduated student number growth.

This is largely due to the availability of long time series of data for a large developing or developed both Asia or foreign countries rather than because it is viewed as preferable to the traditional classroom teacher human captial stock of education measures. So, based on the motivation that online and classroom school enrolment rates conflate online and traditional classroom human capital stock and accumulation effects and lead to misinterpretations of the role of online education labor force growth. It seems online education may be one of method to raise online education human capital and the online graduated student number productivity growth to cause any developed or developing Asia or foreign countries' online education ecommerce economic growth for long term nowadays.

The 21st century educational skills became known as critical thinking, communication, collaboration and creativity. So, every individual student is needed own ability to solve any learning challenges. In the global manufacturing economies that existed 50 years ago, students need own reading, writing and calculation ability to learn easily, even how to gather useful data to prepare to study from internet channel. Because, in modern world, students must be proficient communicators, creators, critical thinkers and collaborators and students need have effort to study these subject areas, including foreign languages, the arts, geography, science, law, business and social studies etc. subjects. It seems internet channel is the sole learning method to let any subject students to gather data to prepare their learning more easily in the short time.

As the same time, due to workforce skills and demands have changed dramatically in the last twenty years, e.g. many labor manufacturing method had change to new technological manufacturing method., even, labor service job will also change to artificical intelligence service job as soon as possible. Moreover, global employers need to employ employees who need have a rapid increase in jobs involving non-routine, analytic and interactive communication skills. Thus, it causes today's job market requires competencies , such as critical thinking and the ability to interact with the company employees from many different cultural backgrounds employee working environment. Thus, students need own these critical thinking and excellent communication skills to prepare to work in society. It seems any country's schools need to teach students these skills to prepare to work in societies. It brings this question: Can internet channel attract students to learn how to use critical thinking mind and attitude to solve their learning difficulty and future working difficulty in any working environment easily?

To answer this question, we need to know what the critical thinking is. Critical thinking and problem solving can be defined as: Using various types of reasoning (inductive, deductive etc.) as appropriate to the situation , using systems thinking to analyze how parts of a whole interact with each other to produce overall outcomes in complex systems; making judgements and decisions in effectively analyzed and evaluated evidence, arguments, claims and belief, analyzing and evaluating major alternative points of view, synthesizing and making connections between information and arguments, interpreting information and drawing conclusion based on the best analysis, reflecting critically on learning experiences of unfamiliar problems in both conventional and innovative ways and identifying and asking significant questions that clarifying various points of view and leading to better solutions (Catalina Foothills School District). Thus, if the university student owned these abilities to learn. I believe that who must feel not difficulties to learn.

Then, it brings this question: How critical thinking and problem solving can be integrated into classroom teaching and learning across a variety of grade levels and disciplines. For art subject student example, music students individually articulate different ways to interpret the same musical passage. Students then compare the various interpretations and determine which one is most effective, taking into account age-appropriate considerations, such as the style of the music. For another world languages student example , with the job title omitted , students read various job/career advertisements and then match the appropriate job title to the ad. Students are divided into groups. Each group is asked to investigate 3 to 5 different career/job sites and identify the jobs and careers that are in high demand in a particular city, region or country. Then, students can present their findings of the most suitable world languages learning method to the class. Next, for science students example, who need to research how the physical and chemical properties of different natural and human designed materials affect their decomposition under various conditions. So, I recommend students can apply internet to gather data to compare their findings to the material evidence used by scientists to reconstruct the lives of past cultures, as well as create a map of their classroom as a future written descriptions of artifacts and what who imply about the cultures, discovered by scientists. So, the science students can be trained to learn how to apply critical thinking to plan and conduct scientific investigations and write detailed explanations based on their evidence when they often apply internet to gather data to compare their findings to the material evidence used by scientists to make judgement to prepare their learning in every lesson.

Thus, the owned critical thinking skillful science students who can compare their explanations to those made by scientists and relate them to their own understandings of the natural and designed world more easily. Finally for social studies students example, in groups , students explore how selected societies for fuel (e.g. England's use of its forests at the beginning of the industrial revolution) and the economic impact of that use. The owned critical thinking skillful social studies students will choose to use videoconference by internet oral communication channel (e.g.

www.skp.com) to collect information from relevant government officials about the use of corn for biofuel instead of food and analyze the environmental and economic implications of this use. For example, after they gather data to find any scientific evidences from internet channel. Then, they can choose to use sound reasoning and relevant scientific evidence examples, who can also analyze the historical evolution of a contemporary public policy issue, place it within a cultural and historical context, and use a online digital publishing tool to report the work from internet channel. In conclusion, above of these learning behaviors, which are the owned critical thinking or skillful students who will choose to decide to do these learning behaviors habitually from internet channel. Also, I feel global schools specially, universities and secondary schools ought train whose students to learn how to use internet channel to gather data to do critical thinking to solve any learning problems easily.

Consequently, due to students will feel online learning can be one kind good learning method to compare traditional classroom learning method. So, it is possible that many students will choose to learn from internet more than classrooms. It will bring the online graduated student number will raise, otherwise, the classroom graduated student number will fall down in the future.

3.1

How online education solve the shortage of graduated student number supply.

Recently, the research indicates the impact of online education quality is mixed by the online student individual learning attitude. Moreover, recent studies actually suggest that online educational institute supply quantity is unrelated to the graduated student number growth at least in developed countries. So, it implies that if the one online education institute can provide excellent online education service to its students to learn. Otherwise, many online education institutes can not provide excellent online education service to their students to learn and let they feel difficult to learn.

Consequently, the one excellent online school can let many students to graduate more than many poor online education institutions. So, the online school number is not the main factor to influence the graduated student number. Otherwise, the online education service performance and online teacher individual teaching experiences and knowledge will be the main factor to influence the graduated student number.

On the other hand, a growing literature focuses on the online graduated student growth impact of online education quality, measures by international test scores. It finds a strong effect of online education quality on online graduated student number growth when confirming that online education supplier quantity is irrelevant apart from via its impact on online education quality.

So, I suggest the developing Asia countries' governments, e.g. China, Korea should continue their market based reforms in online education. For example, by streamlining the requirements and process to establish new free online schools. The goals should be to expand parental choice as widely as possible. Because online education might be way to personal fulfilment, but it can also be an instrument for a healthy online learning economy. So, reforming the online education system could be a key part of any long term graduated student number growth strategy to any Asia developing countries. For example, whose governments can increase spending significantly, when gradually raising the compulsory education age from 16 to 18 age following the online education skills to online teachers and online learning skills to online students both act. Also expanding the average number of years spent in online education be sufficient to improve the online graduated student number growth. Also, any one of Asia developing countries can raise online education quality more important that how much online education one receives , i.e. online education supplier quantity? And how online education policy can secure the highest economic dividend in as reduce efficient manner as possible.

The policy implication is clear the Asia developing countries' governments should encourage an increase in the online stduent enrolment shares of independently operated online teaching schools, for example by streamlining the requirements and process to establish new free online schools. A voucher system with which pupils can attend the online teaching school of their choice, either public or independent would be preferable. Such a system would sharpen competitive incentives in the online education system significantly. Thus increasing the potential for choice to produce an economic dividend.

Why is online education presumed to affect the online graduated student number growth in any one of Asia developing countries? The main reason given is that it should improve the overall online teacher individual skill level, or online teacher human capital of the labor force. Why online teacher human capital teaching skills may be related to the online graduated student number growth.

The reason is because that usually, capital growth is only determined by capital accumulation and technological changes. In the growth model, only technological innovation can explain long term growth because capital accumulation effects suffer from diminishing and returns. Technological change is thus the sole determinant of growth once an economy's new equilibrium/steady state (zero growth states is reached).

At the same time, the sources of technological change, such as online teacher human captial are assumed to be not included as an explanatory variable in the model. In other words, the model treats online education as a residual rather than as integral part of the process of change in explaining an economy's per-capita growth rate. Thus, some economists do not believe traditional classroom education is a conceptual tool to assist the graduated student number growth. However, some economists believe technological change and onlineeducation can assist online graduated student growth when these two factors are same to exist. Thus, online education can impact the online graduated student number growth not only by affecting innovation directly. But also by aiding the adoption of existing technology.

Consequently, the augmented assumed that the effect of online education eventually growth models allow online education at any given level to continue to impact the future graduated student number growth through its effect on technological change and diffusion in the economy. In other meaning, online education can be provide to students to raise high technological human capital to assist economic growth. So, online education can be treated as a regular factor of production to affect the the graduated student number growth rate in the subsequent period.

This has implications for how the online education variable should be included in statistical analyses, which has been a subject of debate. Otherwise, most research has focused mostly on online education supplier quantity,such as the average number of years of online schooling. For example, some older studies used school enrolment rates as a measure of education. Online student nrolment rates impacts are being used different growth periods average over the period. It also indicates that increasing enrolment rates are positive for economic growth in developing Asia countries, e.g. China , Korea etc. In conclusion, it seems online education supply quantity is not the main factor to influence the graduated student number to be raised. Othwise, online education quality is the main factor to influence the online graduated student number growth in long term.

In the future, what kind of subjects will be popular to be accepted to students to choose online learning?Nowadays, science, technology, engineering and mathematics will be popular subjects to any developed countries to be taught by online channel, such as US, UK, Japan as well as developing countries, such as China, India, Hong Kong, Korea growth subjects, even global economic competitiveness and the demand of these subject students will increase to study these subjects in US, even global. Because global many employers will increase demand these qualified workers, due to these qualified workers will have shortage of numbers to supply to global employment market. It trends in k-12 and higher education science and math. Also, preparation coupled with demographic and labor supply trends point to a serious quality of educational worker challenge. Such as, global nations need to increase the supply and quality of knowledge workers whose specialized skills to enable them to work productivity within technology industries and occupations in global. It will bring this question: Can internet technology can raise these Science, technology, engineering and mathematics subjects of teachers' quality of teaching level?

Nowadays, US Department of labor already investing about $14 billion one year in the nation's workforce system and in increasing the science, technology, engineering and math. students' skills and education. So, how to raise student's individual skills to US competitiveness and growth to science, technology , engineering and math. subjects that will be US educational development challenge. Opinion leaders and the publish board agree that education in math. and science is critical to the nation's future success. According to a recent educational testing service survey, it indicated 61% of opinion leaders and 40% of the general publish identify math, science, and technology skills will be the most important ingredients in the nation's strategy to compete in the global economy (Zinth 2006).

Thus, in US , the science, technology, engineering and math. students' multi-faceted education and workforce challenge include: Many students never feel studying these subjects easily, because of inadequate preparation in math. and science or poor teacher quality in their K-12 education systems(ACT 2006). Many who are academically qualified for postsecondary studies in science and math. fields of both the two and four year levels don't pursue those programs. The might be dissuaded by disappointing curricula and course of study, relatively low salary in these professional (American Association Of State College And Universities 2005).

In conclusion, it is the right time to choose online education method to US , even global. These subjects include science, technology, engineering and math. subject teachers can attempt to learn how to apply internet to teach as well as how to teach their students how to apply internet to learn at themselves homes in order to let them to feel to online learn these subjects effectively and easily and conventiently at their homes.

3.2
Future trends in K-12 education challenges

In the future, the school K-12 education general challenges which will be how to teach students apply cloud computering online technology to learn at home. The majority of trends in K-12 education will use technology , such as cloud computing, mobile learning, learning analytics, open content, remote or virtual laboratories are directly related to improved student learning. However, it will have difficulty to achieve technology education to k-12. Because these young students need time to learn how to apply different computer software or high technology equipment to learn. Moreover, the changing uses of technology require that teachers also change their methods of instruction.

Online cloud computing, mobile learning , virtual laboratories, learning analytics, open content and remote technological learning methods which aim to achieve the studying or learning plan to encourage students can direct their own learning. As a result, teachers must shift from being holders and distributors of knowledge to becoming instructional facilitators who encourage students to direct their own learning.

Thus, the challenges of online technological teaching and learning education challenge will be how to achieve to let students feel easy to use technological tools to learn at home conveniently. Several tools are available to support teachers. Such as social learning networks, e-portfolios and cloud computing allow teachers virtually connect and encourage discussion about best practice among teachers. For cloud computing education tool example, it comprises internet-based tools that don't live on an individual device. This flexibility allow for access to materials stored and the cloud at any location. Students can access homework assignments, readings and support materials anywhere, who can connect with the cloud.

Commonly used examples of cloud computing sharing devices are drop box and google drive. Also, cloud computing is popular in distance learning programs for obvious reasons. There are three categories of cloud computing that may be useful to k-12 educators (Nagel, D. 2013) indicated it includes infrastructure -as-a-service (i.e. virtualization). This category describes scalable virtual machines, bandwidth and storage capacities, platform-as-a-service (Pass). This category describes the environment in which the development and delivery of applications occurs and software-as-a-service (psas). This category describes software that is created for a specific organization's unique needs. Thus, k-12 students need to spend time to learn what are these category difference, then who can choose to use what may or method to use cloud computing to learn more easily in four years.

In fact, K-12 education students will feel difficult how to apply cloud coumputing technology to learn at home. So, it brings this question: Why k-12 students need to apply cloud computing to learn. The reason is mobile technologies have also attracted the attention of high profile educational publishers, such as person, e-books, e-magazines publishers and interactive textbook have optimized for mobile platforms and devices and can easily replace heavier traditional textbooks. It also allow children to interact with material using simple fingers swipes and pinches, which eliminates the need for detailed instructions. It seems it has one day detailed instructions and electronic books will be popular to let any young students to accept to study, such as primary and high school and university students who can learn from computers or mobiles in future one day. Thus, it is the right time k-12 students to learn how to apply technology to learn.

Anyway, distance or distributed e-learning education is one of the most complex issues facing higher education institutions today. However, there are much challenge to education k-12 students by learning. How can teachers teach k-12students by distance education, e-learning or distributed learning method to achieve the effective learn outcome? Is it an extensive of the k-12 classroom or replacement leave? Distance learning is a subject of distributed learning, focusing on k-12 students who may be separated in time and space from their pears and the instructor. Distributed learning can occur either on or off campus, providing k-12 students with greater flexibility and eliminating time as a barrier to learning, campus or online. There are many implications of technology into education , i.e. in making learning distributed . So, the challenge indicates k-12 students to learn how to allocate time to learn from distance learning technology method. For example, eating time, sleeping time, doing homework time and learning time allocation. Teachers need teach students how to arrange and allocate time to learn or sleep or do homwork effectively and easily.

3.3 Distance learning online education challenges

Common assumptions online eduction challenges about higher education include: schools know the student profile and learner preferences for learning and service delivery, student credit hours and full time equivalents are relevant units of measure in distributed education, completion of the curriculum is the measure of competency, traditional institutional models (e.g. for classroom instruction, governance and financing) will be successful in an e-learning educational method, higher education must provide all components of the educational process (e.g. content, curriculum, services and credentialing), external providers of educational services (e.g. courses or tutoring from an internet start-up) are bad or of lower quality than educational institutions, quality is better in a not-for-profit educational organization than in a for profit one, high education will be driven out low quality from bad online education influence, distributed learning is a variable option for all post-secondary education institutions, the faculty member is the focal point od the learning process.

So, all higher education institutions must develop their own distributed learning programs. Although, these assumptions characteristic are good, but which may not all apply to distance distributed learning. Some educational organizations have either inadequate or inappropriate for distributed learning. For example, the nation of credit for seat time has sustained current model of higher education, but will it suffice for a future represented by distributed learning?

However, online technological education will bring these negative influences to students. What are the challenges in influence students psychology from information age mind set? When students often use computer or laptop to learning , constant connectivity, they will reduce time to communicate or make close relationship with whose friends and family at any time and from any place. Then, every online learning student behavior and value will be influences, such as: computers aren't technology only. It is whose part of life, the internet is better than TV reality is no longer real, doing is more important than knowing, trial-and-error, experimentation is preferable to logic , multitasking is a way of life, typing is preferable to handwriting, staying online learning connected is essential every day.

There is zero tolerance for online on-line learning time delays. Thus, the way, schools must organize their educational institutions to change educational method to achieve online learning time and private entertainment time to be balances to every student. Although, online education can give convenient and fast speed to gather information benefits to young students to study. But, educators need to consider these online education challenges which, online educational students will encounter , such as : What kind of support to faculty needs to develop engaging and empowering online environment? Are educators using the unique capabilities of the web to make learning environments engaging and effective? Do educators know which students will learn best of a distance and those for whom it is a poor choice? Thus, it brings this question: Does distributed learning support a specific strategic goal for the educational institutions or is the rationale?

To gain the commitment of all those who must support a major initiative (board , executive cabinet, faculty, teaching staff etc.) , it is important to articulate clearly the strategic goals behind the institution's interest in distributed learning. For example, which is the institution's commitment to educational access? Would distributed education enhance the fulfilment of that goal? Will it seem inconsistent with policies on selectivity and/or the importance of the residential experience? Does distributed education complement educational institution's mission, culture and historic strengths? Do the institutions have clear rationale for distributed eduaction?

Corporate learners work for corporations and are seeking education to maintain or the employing corporation and not by the individual acting alone. Professional enhancement learners are seeking to advance careers or shift careers. They are working adults who make the educational purchasing decision on their own. Degree-completion adult learners are working to complete a degree at an older age . They frequently are working adults who must balance work and family needs with their educational goals. College experience learners are preparing for life , e.g. the traditional students. This segment includes many of the 18 to 24 year old residential college students for whom the coming age process is almost as important as academic achievement. Finally, I shall suggest pre-college (k-12) learners are interested in doing degree level work prior to the completion of high school. This learner age segment may be interested and is more acceptable in getting studying to compare other learnerage segment from internet learning channel.

Consequently, science, engineering, etc. subjects will be online learning popular subjects. Online education will be one method to solve graduated student shortage challenge to supply to these subject employers in societies.

3.4 Online education improves Asia student learning performance

Human capital has ability and efficiency of labor to transform raw materials and capital into products and services to affect economic growth. The accumulation of human capital improves labor productivity and increases the returns to capital. However, a well educated background is essential to raise technology to develop economic growth in Asia developing countries especially.

In macro and micro economic view, the well educated labor (human capital) is often as one of the critical factors to influence rapid economic growth to the Asia developing countries' any regions or cities. Because any of these Asia developing countries, such as China, Korea, Philippines etc. countries which need have well educated and knowledgeable labors to raise any employers' productivities and income growth. So productivity and education factor which ought have close relationship to cause the good or bad economic growth in these any one of Asia developing countries. For example, China was an major industrial and farming country between 1960 year and 2000 year. However, after 2000 year, it began to achieve any commercial investment to raise GDP income and to raise more service provision nature of employment chance to domestic labors. e.g. financial investment, shares trading, hotels and tourism and airlines and restaurants and cinemas etc. service nature businesses commercial investment. Moreover, the foreign investors were also attracted to set up factories to manufacture their products in China's country any area locations. It was possible that this foreign investors felt China's workers' wages were more cheaper than themselves domestic worker wages. For example, USA has the minimum wage legislation to protect it's domestic individual worker wage level. Otherwise, China's individual worker wage level is compared to be paid more lower level to compare to USA's minimual legislative individual worker wage level nowadays. It seems China, Korea, Philippines etc. Asia developing countries need have well educated labors to help them to develop economic growth. Because the developed countries' foreign well educated labors, e.g. USA, UK etc. who feel whose countries can give the best salary compensation level and benefits to let them to support to work and to live in whose countries. So the developed countries' well educated labors won't choose to go to China to work very easily.

It seems those developing Asia countries which governments need to invest in education sector to increase many knowledgeable human labors capital to assist them to raise whose technological productivity or service productivity or factory productivity to achieve economic growth for long term. If any one of these Asia developing Asia countries still want to keep the competitive position in global environment in the future. So, these Asia developing countries must need good education to train any aspects of high knowledgeable labors to supply to themselves society to work in essential.

How online education is suitable to Japan education

Ha, Kim and Lee (2009) provided evidence to indicate that "using panel data covering from 1989 year to 2000 year in Japan, Korea and Taipei, China as the distance to the technology frontier narrows basis research and development (R&D) investment, i.e. highly skilled labor which showed the higher growth effect than development R&D investment , i.e. less skilled labor. They also provided evidence that the quality of tertiary education has a significantly positive effect on the productivity of R&D.

Nowadays, education is commonly regarded as the most direct influence to people out of poverty owing to the tendency for employment opportunities especially for higher skilled workers to be created in Asia developing countries. In fact, raising productivity is depended on the quantity and quality of human resource, which itself largely depends on investment in education theoretical linkages between education and growth. Generally, growth theory suggests that economic growth depends on the accumulation of economic, including human assets and the return on these assets, which depend on technological progress, the efficiency which assets are being used. So, growth theory which emphasizes on the centrality of human capital for innovation and technological progress. However, the theory indicates of policy ineffectiveness which characterizes the neo-classical growrh theory by giving importance to the production of new technologies and human capital development. So focusing on factors within the model rather than relying on external factors. It seems the economists of supporting growth believe that improvements in productivity are linked to a faster pace of innovation and extra investment in human capital. Also these economists of supporting growth theory emphasize on the need for governments and private sector educational institutions and job markets for tertiary students' demand and to innovate knowledgeable of social economy to actively provide incentives for individual student to become inventive in any countries. They also identify the central role of knowledge as determinant of economic growth. Hence, growth theory can predict positive externalities and spillover effects from development of a high valued-added knowledge economy to the development and maintenance of a competitive advantage across the global.

Why do I research the relationship between education and productivity can influence the economic growth to Asia developing countries? Although, human capital includes education, health and aspects of social capital. The main focus of the present study is on education. The analysis stresses the distination between the quantity of education measured by years of attainment at various levels and the quality measured by scores on internationally comparable examinations, e.g. China education and Korea education comparision. In fact, the global long term economic growth was the central macroeconomic problem and it was fortunately accompanied in the late 1980 year by importance advances in the theory of economic growth. This period featured the development of global growth models, in which the long term rate of growth was determined within the model.

A key feature of these models is a theory of technological progress, viewed as a process whereby purposeful research and application lead over time to new and better products and methods of production by developed economic globalization. The recent growth models are useful for understanding why advanced economies and the world is as whole, can continue to grow in the long run despite the workings of diminishing returns in the accumulation of physical and human capital. These countries include, e.g. America, England which are observed to be rich and high tend also to be those that have high long run target levels of per high capita output in a setting that includes human capital and technological change. So education is also essential to raise labour knowledge and technological level to assist developed countries, e.g. USA, UK , to raise productivity to achieve economic growth. So, the developed or developing countries' both government policies and education institutions need to concern their national population to arrange the different primary, secondary and tertiary educational policy to educate to develop whose students to develop different professional and knowledgeable and skillful abilities to already develop their careers in different nature of jobs to enter their societies to work nowadays. However, if we were the identify how education contributes to cause economic growth in any Asia developing countries. We need to compare states that have a similar distance to the frontier and yet choose difference pattern of investment in education. For example, building a new school for a research university, the process is when a vacancy arises on an committee that controls expenditure. Because governments and universities need to concern what the labour market demand, so the research university can decide prefer to choose what kinds of subjects to be taught to its potential students, e.g. medical or architect or law or engineering or business or social science, computer science etc. subjects among of them subjects, which subjects will be chosen to be taught to its potential students preferably. So, the job demand market research is very important because it can help the research university to choose what the preferable subjects will be demanded to supply to the labour market increasing in any one of Asia developing countries within future three or five years.

Theories of economic growth have emphasised the role of human capital which may affect economic growth. Human capital is as an extra input in the aggregate production function, where the output of the means economy is a direct function of factor inputs: physical capital, labor and human capital. However, technologies can raise innovate capacity of economy through developing new ideas. So, education was seemed that it could be raised graduated students' abilities to raise productivity to any one of Asia developing countries by high technological skill.

How online education improve Asia students learning attitude

Any countries have two different channels through which human capital can affect long run economic growth by education provision. The first channel is when human capital is a direct input in the production function and the second channel is when the human capital affects the technology parameter. The result establishes a long run relationship between education and economic growth. A well educated labour force appears to significantly influence economic growth both as a factor in the production function and through total factor productivity. With its large resources of human and natural resources, the potential to build a prosperous economy to reduce poverty significantly and to provide the health, education services that its population needs. As the Asia developing countries, e.g. China or Korea, which are poor countries past years, which need foreign investors' different businesses development in their countries. So, themselves education is commonly regarded as the most direct avenue to rescue a substantial number of people out of poverty since there is likely to be more employment opportunities and higher wages for skilled workers. Furthermore, education can enable children's attitudes and assists them to grow up with social values that are more benefitical to their nations and themselves.

The theoretical basis of education on economic growth is rooted in the endogenous growth theory. Endogenous growth economists believe that improvements in productivity can be linked to a faster pace of innovation and extra investment in human capital. Engogenous growth theorists argue the need for government and private sector institutions and markets which need to innovate and provide incentives for individuals to be inventive. There is also a central role for knowledge as a determinant of economic growth theory can predict positive externalities and spill over effects from development of a high valued-added knowledge economy which is able to develop and maintain a competitive advantage in growth industries in the global economy.

Nowadays, education at levels countries to economic growth through imparting general attitudes and discipline and special skills necessary for a variety of work places. It contirbutes to economic growth by improving health, reducing fertility and possibly by contributing to political stability to different developing or developed both countries. The major importance of the educational system to any labor market would depend majority in ability to produce a literate, disciplines, flexible labor force via high quality education. Consequently, with economic development new technology is applied to production with results in an increase in the demand for workers and better education. In the developing countries, e.g. China, Korea, rich individuals allocate labor time not only for their own production and knowledge accumulation, but also train the poor individuals. In the past, some economists estimated a model of economic growth and human capital accumulation based on a sample of developing countries, e.g. China, Korea etc. are not a different stage of development. Their result revealed that the increase in the primary and secondary countries to an increase in productivity. They indicate that human capital acccumulation rates are affected by demographic variables. For example, they established that an increase in life expectancy at birth brings about an increase in secondary and tertiary education when a decrease in the dependence rate negatively affects secondary education. Finally, they added that geographic variables have a considerable importance in the human capital accumulation process. Nevertheless, studies differed on the impact of human capital on productivity.

The economists also indicate that human capital accumulation rates are affected by demographic variables as well as the increase in the primary and secondary level of education contibutes to an increase in productivity. For example, they established that a increase in life expectancy at birth brings about an increase in secondary and tertiary education when a decrease in the dependence rate negatively affects secondary education. However, who also believe the overall results of secondary and higher education can have a significant positive impact on growth, when primary education had not contributed to economic growth.

The GDP per unit of labor input should be related to the share of labor of a particular type (graduates or workers at different qualification levels) weighted by the average human capital of the type of worker (captured by the relative wages of different types of labor input). It seems measure of the relationship between education and productivity and economic growth can be quantified clearing to developing Asia any countries.

In past, the EUKLEMS project indicated key findings of 15 developed countries for one economic report: GDP per employment hour increased from 1992 year to 2005 year, the highest annual average percentage change was in Finland (2.7%), Japan (2.5%) and the UK (2.4%). These countries had the lowest level of GDP per employment hour in 1982 year, when the period considered the Netherlands and the USA had the highest GDP employment hour. Also it indicated the share of employment with tertiary education also increased from 1982 year to 2005 year in all countries. The highest annual average percentage change was in Australia (5%) followed by the UK (4.9%). Both of these countries had relatively low shares of employment with tertiary education in 1982 year at 6%, compared with 22.1% in the USA and 18.7% in Finland. The large increased closed the gap, but the USA and Finland still had higher employment shares with tertiary education than Australia and the UK in 2005 year. The economic report also indicatd that a 1% increase in the share of the workforce with a university degree raises the level of long run productivity by 0.2%-0.5%. So, it implied the education and productivity has close relationship to developed countries also. However, the economic benefits, both to the individual and to the wider economy of a university degree with clearly depend on the quality and skills to developing and developed countries both.

So, improvement in educational outcomes have been widely recognised as essential in enhancing growth in both developed and developing countries. In fact, education is acquire by individuals provide social returns at the macroeconomic level and addition indirect benefits to economic growth.

Firstly, I suppose it has relationship between online educational teacher human resource its human resource capital and online education method has close relationship to cause economic growth to any developed or developing countries both nowadays. Because if human capital and education factor has close relationship to influence any country's economic growth, then it is possible to cause productivity and economic growth has close relationship. However, some economists indicate the evidence on the relationship between human capital and economic growth and who conclude that there is strong evidence that human capital increases productivity. Suggesting that education really is productivity-enhancing, rather than education is used by individuals to signal their ability to potential employers.

The primary measures are used to capture the average level of human capital per worker include:

I. The average number of years of schooling of the workforce or population, which assumes a linear relationship with human capital.

II. The share of the workforce population with specific educational qualifications.

III. School enrolment rates, specially as a starting value. This flow into education is often used as stock of qualifications and is available for developed Asia countries, e.g. Hong Kong, Japan and developing Asia countries, e.g. China, Korea both.

However, developing Asia countries have potential problems arising from measurement errors in education, as the average schooling levels are derived from enrolment flows. They adopt more reliable country level education micro data and find a positive result or response between the growth rate of education and economic growth. Human capital flows are most commonly provided by school enrolment rates, have been widely used in studies of the relationship between human captial and growth. This is largely due to the availability of long time series of data for a large developing or developed both Asia or foreign countries rather than because it is viewed as proferable to the human captial stock of education measures. So, based on the motivation that school enrolment rates conflate human capital stock and accumulation effects and lead to misinterpretations of the role of labor force growth. It seems education may be one of method to raise human capital and productivity growth to cause any developed or developing Asia or foreign countries' economic growth for long term nowadays.

How online education increases graduated student number in developing Asia countries.

Recently, the research indicates the impact of education quality is mixed. Moreover, recent studies actually suggest that education quantity is unrelated to economic growth at least in developed countries. On the other hand, a growing literature focuses on the growth impact of education quality, measures by international test scores. It finds a strong effect of education quality on economic growth when confirming that education quantity is irrelevant apart from via its impact on quality. So, I suggest the developing Asia countries' governments, e.g. China, Korea should continue their market based reforms in education. For example, by streamlining the requirements and process to establish new free schools. The goals should be to expand parental choice as widely as possible. Because education might be way to personal fulfilment, but it can also be an instrument for a healthy economy. So, reforming the education system could be a key part of any long term growth strategy to any Asia developing countries. For example, whose governments can increase spending significantly, when gradually raising the compulsory education age from 16 to 18 age following the education and skills act. Also expanding the average number of years spent in education be sufficient to improve growth. Also, any one of Asia developing countries can raise education quality more important that how much education one receives , i.e. education quantity? And how education policy can secure the highest economic dividend in as reduce efficient manner as possible. The policy implication is clear the Asia developing countries' governments should encourage an increase in the enrolment shares of independently operated schools, for example by streamlining the requirements and process to establish new free schools. A voucher system with which pupils can attend the school of their choice, either public or independent would be preferable. Such a system would sharpen competitive incentives in the education system significantly. Thus increasing the potential for choice to produce an economic dividend.

Why is education presumed to affect economic growth in any one of Asia developing countries? The main reason given is that it should improve the overall skill level, or human capital of the labor force. How human capital may be related to economic growth. Usually, capital growth is only determined by capital accumulation and technological changes. In the growth model, only technological innovation can explain long term growth because capital accumulation effects suffer from diminishing and returns. Technological change is thus the sole determinant of growth once an economy's new equilibrium/steady state (zero growth states is reached. At the same time, the sources of technological change, such as human captial are assumed to be not included as an explanatory variable in the model. In other words, the model treats education as a residual rather than as integral part of the process of change in explaining an economy's per-capita growth rate. Thus, some economists do not believe education is a conceptual tool to assist economic growth. However, some economists believe technological change and education can assist economic growth when these two factors are same to exist. Thus, education can impact growth not only by affecting innovation directly. But also by aiding the adoption of existing technology.

The augmented assumed that the effect of education eventually growth models allow education at any given level to continue to impact growth through its effect on technological change and diffusion in the economy. In other meaning, education can be provide to students to raise high technological human capital to assist economic growth. So, education can be treated as a regular factor of production to affect the growth rate in the subsequent period. This has implications for how the education variable should be included in statistical analyses, which has been a subject of debate. Otherwise, most research has focused mostly on education quantity,such as the average number of years of schooling. For example, some older studies used school enrolment rates as a measure of education. Enrolment rates impacts are being used different growth periods average over the period. It also indicates that increasing enrolment rates are positive for economic growth in developing Asia countries, e.g. China , Korea etc. In conclusion, it seems education quantity and quality as well as productivity has also relationship to influence developing Asia countries' economic growth for long term.

3.5 Choosing overseas university learning challenge

University campus location choice challenge.

Whether University location can be a competitive advantage to attract students to study? The school (university) location means that the proximity of city center and the proximity of students home. To increase the occupancy rate, the university location is needed to provide as a model and resources based view which will be used to explain why the school location is a kind of competitive advantage for universities. According to Porter theory, it is a part of factor, which has some advantages against the treat of entry. It can decrease the treatment of rivalry. However, a good place has a certainly positive effect for attracting staff and more students. For resource-based view, the location is one of the internal resources. It can be accepted as one of the physical and tangible resource of a university.

I shall apply the first attractive factor of Porter five forces and resource based model to analyze my opinion to explain why school (university location) can influence students to choose the university to study. This view is represented by the opportunities and the threats. The university of thought is the resource based view which is represented by the strengths and weaknesses of the firm. Porter's five force model of competition elements include threats of entrants or substitutes, bargaining power of buyers or suppliers and competition rivalry. A firm's resources include brand name, in-house knowledge of technology, employment of skilled personnel, trade contract, machinery, efficient procedures and capital etc. Such as, both tangible and intangible assets are considered a firm's resources. For a university, customers can be thought as a students, suppliers can be thought as staff. In higher education industry, the good transportation infrastructure and well-connected universities have some advantages against the treat of entry to attract good staff and more students. The place of a university can decrease of treatment of rival and a good place has certainty positive location is an opportunity for universities to attract the students.

The resource based theory of university location competitive advantage challenge
According to the Porter's theory, the resource based theory can apply competitive resources to be identifies to higher education institutions. For higher education institutions, such as resources might include the reputation of certain departments, the grouping together of areas of specialist expertise and the development of technical patents etc. Also higher education resources may not be imperfectly mobile, as the competitive resources of a university identifies tangible, intangible and organizational assets. So, the tangible resources might include campus location, building capacity, conference facilities and medical research facilities. Intangible resources generally include such items as patents, teaching and research performance, service levels and technology and the geographical location of a service. In a university, such intangible resources might include some of the above and may also include employees/ associates, e.g. experienced professors, renowned authors and distinguished teachers. Also, the location of a university can be accepted as physical and tangible resources of a university. However, I believe location is shown as an important

factor to affect the students' university enrolment selection decisions.

To sources of competitive advantages are thought to be the reputation of the institution, the curriculum and educational standards, school fees (tuition), location and student activities etc. different factors. Moreover, any university's general client segments include such as, high school graduates, elderly students and international students, that have been influenced by several factors when selecting the best university to study. One of these factors is again location, the proximity to home and easy transportation is critical factor in selecting a university. Presumably, institutions that are located along well-established public transit routes have a competitive advantage over those with poor transit links. Due to the efficiency of innovation activity increased in easily accessible locations with a high density of economic activity. The existence of education and research institutions as well as easily available information is suggested as a reason for this increase. Also private higher education institutions desire to benefit from these flows by locating itself nearby. Therefore, together with other factors, such as existing capital global flows should be existing capital and population, level of income and location decisions of foundation universities. The location, social life campus, proximity of campus to the city center, exchange programs, the curricula infrastructure, languages medium of instruction and activities are the most significant factors to influence students to choose which university to study. By the past statistic indicated that the location has 94% rate, the proximity of campus to the city center has 84% rate. So, it seems the proximity of campus to the city center factor is more prior choice to compare with the school location is close to the student home factor.

Huang (2012) stated that " the right location attracts more students and ensures the revenues of the institution. The location of an educational institution might influence its future prospect of growth. A good location attracts not only more students, but also excellent teaching staff". Because of job opportunities areas, the students are able to get a part-time job and earn extra money for their tuition (Huang, 2012). Marketing concept has four "P", it can apply to university educational business, such as educational promotion, tuition price, teachers of people and school campus location of place.

Finally, I shall give two assumptions to explain why if the university location is not popular to be accepted to the country's students in general, then it will cause who won't choose to study the university. However, even if the university's tuition is reasonable or cheaper or lecturers are famous or reputation or educational advertisement is attractive. In fact, the poor location factor will influence many local or overseas students who don't choose to study the university in the country. The first assumption is that most of students feel that the proximity of the university to the city center factor affects their university final choice decision and the another assumption is that most of students feel that the proximity of university to home affects their university final choice decision. There two assumptions are used to determine the importance of university location to attract the students. In Porter theory, either proximity of city center and/or proximity of student's home of a university factors have same advantages against the treat of entry. It can decrease the treatment of rival and a good place has certainly positive effect to attract teaching staff and more students. In resource based view, the location can be accepted a kind of internal resources. It can be accepted as one of the sustainable competitive advantages literature, location is a kind of advantage for higher education institutions.

Alternative modes of course delivery chanllenge

The factor of student demand for alternative modes of course delivery is another factor to influence the student who chooses the university to study. Any university's educational program includes program design, material production (both print and e-version), promotion, essay competition, school networks, budgeting, coordinating with various constructors, data base management and program evaluation etc.

Nowadays, university teaching methods may include face-to face, online and hybrid modes of course delivery. However, the several ways to students to deliver their course works ,such as full time, part time, internal/ non campus, external studies/distance education, summer school, winter school, semester study and trimester study. The multi site of a university , e.g. major provider of distance online education operates popular affordable learning for student to use internet to study. Although, students do not need to attend to university classroom to listen lecturer's teaching, but it can reduce face-to-face contact between lecturers and students in university classroom often.

Although, it is a technological and innovative and effective learning modalities. In fact, such new technological teaching modalities may be necessitated to the graduated or master degree or doctoral degree students. But, I feel the online teaching method is not suitable to the bachelor degree students. As the delivery of course content or the commoditization of knowledge must be re-thought to the bachelor's if the student can't enquire whose lecturer any questions to give feedback by face-to-face. Then, who will concern the course to feel more difficult possibly if who can't listen whose lecturer's opinion to solve whose challenges about the course any questions immediately in classroom often.

The second attractive factor of student demand for alternative modes of course delivery is another factor to influence the student who chooses the university to study. Nowadays, university teaching method include face to face, online and hybrid modes of course delivery. However, the several ways to students to deliver their coursework, such as full time, part time, internal/on campus, external studies/distance education, "summer school, winter school, semester study and trimester study." The multi site of a university, e.g. major popular provider of distance online education operates a flexible learning for student to use internet to study. It can reduce face to face contact between teachers and students into university classrooms. Although, it is a technological and innovative and effective learning modalities. In fact, such new technological teaching modalities may be necessitated to the graduated students or master degree or doctoral degree students. But, I feel the online teaching method is not suitable to the bachelor degree students. As the delivery of course content or the commoditization of knowledge must be re-thought to the bachelor degree students because whose knowledge level is limited if the student can't ask whose lecturer any questions by face to face contact. So, students will feel difficult to learn if who can't listen whose lecturers' teaching and to enquire any questions and to give feedback in classrooms immediately. It is possible that who will wait long time to ask many questions to prepare to wait lecturers to give feedback by email later if their lecturers use online teaching method. So it is essential that educators and administrators need to understand differentiated teaching demand to different knowledge level of students. Because student preferences may vary by age, cultural, background, degree types, learning style and matter etc. factors to decide whether whose students are suitable to teach by either online distance learning method between individual student and whose computer or face to face learning method between students and the lecturer in classroom face to face oral teaching educational method. In fact, working adults remain strongly associated either interest in online delivery. However, the availability of evening/weekend choices is the second most important enrollment factor to adult students, due to who consider when enrolling in an institution to indicate the important of face-to-face traditional delivery at not convenient times. So, online education is most clearly suited to independent learners those individuals who are self-motivated and self reliant and those who have a problem solving orientation.

The 2006 year Education Inventions survey found that students interested in associate, bachelor's and master's degrees were most open to whole online delivery, although who were also open to campus-based delivery. Similarly, Gartner's 2008 year e-learning survey found that complete graduate programs offered online continue online. For example, international student demand for

Australian higher education is expected to exceed supply in 2020 year, and key 2025 year there will be a shortfall of 22,692 international places on projected demand of 290,848. There numbers imply that to meet demand, Australian universities may want to invest further in online degree/delivery options. However, recent statistics indicate dealing interest in fully online programs in South East Asia, and a survey of 469 transnational students in 2007 year found that a majority of students opposed online provision. These findings suggest that, when branch campuses are found to be prohibitively expensive, the future of transnational programs is in programs that include face-to-face interaction facilitated by an offshore partner of the educational provider. However, education consumers prefer to combine online delivery and geographical proximity. Some of students who are living close to university campus. So who can access to courses delivered in a traditional mode, but chose to take online courses for the flexibility to it afforded them. This is an increasing trend in U.S. institutions as well, whereas online courses are used to cater solely to non-traditional students at a long distance from the campus, increasingly such classes are made available to the mainstream student constituency.

Online and hybrid courses teaching challenge

How can the technology online teaching contributing improve student outcome? At least, learning outcomes for students in online and hybrid courses match those of students in traditional settings. When these are reasons to believe that the hybrid model would produce more effective learning outcomes than the fully-online model in theory. Also evidence suggests that e-learning continues to grow in popularity with the number of hybrid or blended courses increasing at the fastest rate, although online/hybrid courses certainly do not outcomes courses presented the traditional (i.e. face-to-face traditional classroom) delivery method. These facts help to demonstrate that despite the popularity and increased availability of online courses. However, students still value traditional classroom methods and that online options may not significantly detract from on-campus enrollments.

Hybrid degree programs, also known as blended programs are courses of study that combine traditional classroom based instruction with significant amounts of online instruction, with each passing semester, hybrid degree programs become increasingly popular for students and universities alike. Such courses allow students to reduce time-consuming trips to campus when still benefiting from face-to-face teaching method allow colleges and universities to more effectively use classroom space and to reduce cost. For these reasons, hybrid courses are often praised as the best of both classroom and online teaching methods, it is possible that students have chance to go to classroom to listen lecturer's teaching and who also have chance to use internet to learn from online teaching method as the same time. These is no standard model for hybrid education. Some programs may have students split their time evenly between online and on-campus instruction; some may have students complete the majority of their work online with occasional intensive weekends of on-campus activity and some require students to enroll in a combination of traditional classes as well as strictly online classes. Nowadays, a major educational consulting group found that hybrid or blended learning was the most rapidly growing delivery option when online, hybrid and traditional delivery options were taken into acount. Because of the trend towards more hybrid programming, university officials concern on their potential impact on enrollment levels for on-campus degree programs. Some speculate that hybrid programs have the potential to overtake traditional programs, when others hope to use hybrid programs as stepping stones to attract more students to campus on a full time basis. The structures of different programs reflect institutions' intent to use hybrid programs to attract students from non-traditional areas. For example, Michigam State university's Master of social work hybrid program accepts roughly 25 students per year. In 2008 year, these students lived anywhere from 85 to 435 miles from the main campus, therefore frequent in person activities were not feasible. Gather in addition to completing online assignments, students attended a one-week-summer institute on campus in June and face-to-face instruction sessions in smaller groups organized by geography once per month during the fall and spring semesters. In short, hybrid programs do not necessarily replace on-campus offerings, nor do they commonly draw more students to campus on a full time basis. Rather, they complement existing program offerings by reaching out to new packets of students who have the mean to visit campus on occasion but not regularly.

In conclusion, any university ought follow its subjects, student age, school location and tuition, lecturers' reputation and school research facilities etc. factors to decide whether the course is suitable to be chose either online teaching or face-to-face traditional classroom teaching or hybrid (online and face-to-face both) teaching method to teach whose different degree level students. Because these factors will influence who to choose which kind of subjects to study. For example, if many first year students feel the subjects are difficult to learn. It implies that online distance teaching or hybrid teaching method is not suitable to be taught to them. The traditional face-to-face contact traditional classroom teaching method is more suitable to be taught to them. So, it is flexible to any one of these teaching method to choose to teach any subjects to university student. It is no absolute suitable teaching method to teach any one of subject in any one of university. Because any university is independent, it means that the teaching method is suitable to be taught to the students in the university. It doesn't mean that the same teaching method is suitable to be taught to the students to another university because every university's lecturer's reputation, school tuition fee, course's contents and qualities and student age segment and location is different among of them. It is very difficult to ensure which kind of teaching method must be suitable to be taught to the subject to all universities in any countries.

The third attractive factor is concerned how to manage student experience in university life. It is as the totality of a student's interaction with institution. How university management decisions on operational matters are affecting the student individual experience to attract who to study, rather than on teaching and learning activities. University learning experience can decide into those components: the application experience; covering the interactions between potential student and the institutions, up to the point of arrival; the academic experience; students' interactions with the institution associated with their studies, excluding for these purposes teaching and learning processes; the campus experience. Because student life not directly connected with study, which may include activities away from the actual campus and the graduate experience. However, any university's role ought to assist students' transition to employment, instead of education aim.

I shall explain whether this university life experience factors will influence student individual university enrolment choice to study. The management of the student experience is in institutional terms at the heart of responses to their new radically uncertain environment, the externally-driven changes have led to significant new university experience changes in the university structures, policies and processes, resulting in changed institutional cultures. These changes have occurred in different ways depending on the type of university. The research questions that are: Are changes in the higher education leading to change institutional types? Which managerial approaches appear to be the most effective in leading to enhance student experiences and why?

In general, centralizing services, standard
in procedures and strengthening management controls trend to remove discretion at departmental level in the managing experience university. For example, large university can seek to use existing institutional cultures to encourage greater concern for students' needs on the part of both academic and professional staffs. Although, organizational change will happen, it usually will take

the form of changing the reporting lines of student related services to create more coherent functional groupings, rather than comprehensive reorganizations. However, a cultural shift in the direction of improving the student experience, in several dimensions regardless of institutional types.

Similarly, whether the university can provide well recruitment service for graduates, this factors can improve the competitive positions in the terms of graduated student recruitment service experience. The cultural shift includes an increased emphasis on employability, new emphasis includes employment-related curriculum changes and enhanced support for recruitment advice and placements, it is concerned to achieve good results for graduated student employment. There is a sense that is focused in response. In believe to student demands on immediate employment rather than on longer term career possibilities. Also, competitive pressure and the consequential need to enhance the support given to student life have led to the introduction of measures to enhance the attractiveness and utility of campuses in various ways. These often utility of campuses in various ways. These often involve library/learning resources improvements, with extended hours of access and the creation of social learning spaces.

However, the different institutional responses to the changing environment that can be detected support the view whether that ideas of effectiveness to institutionally determined. Whether the student university experience can influence who chooses to study the university. So, I shall indicate these research questions, such as: Are changes in higher education leading to changes institutional policies and practices which affect the student experience? Are there differences according to institutional types? Which managerial approaches appear to be the most effective in leading to enhance student experiences and why?

It is important to acknowledge that each student's set of experiences with be unique to that person. However, institutionally intended patterns of the student experience , in areas over which institutions can have some influence. The experience is concerned on student (non-learning) experience. the experiences of student has different respects, mostly in terms of teaching and learning for the particular classes of students (part time, mature, international students). For example, student journey experience can have these elements: First contact and admission, pre-arrival, arrival and orientation, induction, reorientation and reintroduction to study for continuing students and induction preparing to leave, graduation and beyond. Students need to feel satisfaction when who enroll to the university at the first day. The matters, who will contact on the university orientation day. Such as travel to the university accesses to facilities (libraries, computing, student support, teaching and learning, social life and self-development and finance). Because student expectations are variable and unpredictable and because it is not obvious that students are always the best judges of whatever is defined as quality, particularly were academic judgement is involved.

However, the university customer (student satisfaction) vs quality argument is in a traditional relationship. For example, the university service quality includes libraries and IT (information technology) facilities which are closely associated will teaching and learning activities and where academic priorities tend to be bound up with institutional requirement about efficiency and effectiveness. Other university services, such as catering and accommodation are operated on what might be considered to be supplied and demand based commercial principles: Students are indeed the customers of these services. Other student facing services, such as admissions academic administration , student advice and support and careers guidance are not operated on commercial principles in the usual sense of the term but clearly provide services to student and potential and former student, even if these users are not customers in the strictest sense. This is because unlike with catering or student accommodation, there is not an alternative university registry to which students can dissatisfy with the service on offer. Nor are direct payments from users practicable for most of these services. Instead of quality of teaching, students hope a strong emphasis on student social life, the campus environment, accommodation and other non-academic matters.

Also the elements of the student journey service can influence the university student enrollment numbers. First, the application experience covers the interacting between potential students ad institution up to the point of arrival, Second, the academic experience students' interactions with the institution associated with the students, excluding these purposes teaching and learning processes. Finally, the campus experience, student life not connected with study, which may include activities away from the actual campus. Also the graduate students experience, the institution's role is assisting students' transition on employment. For example, all universities can find open days to be valuable recruitment exercises to attract more visitors to applications. The open day can give them a taste of university life and to help in managing their expectations. Potential students frequently used social media sites to obtain more information. As a result, a paid graduate interim, managed by the central marketing department is placed in each academic department with the task of fielding face book and twitter queries from potential and current students . So senior managers need to consider communication with prospective students as a crucial stage in the student journey experiences. Effective communication may reduce the number of students who drop out in their first year. This often happen, it is thought because students come with mistaken expectations that might have been corrected through more effective communications. It is noted, generally that student using these technologies expected instant expense. The management task for the student admissions experience now involves greater emphasis on the presentation of the university, both before and during visits by potential students and their parents more effort given to the induction of students and the management of their expectations and a need to response rapidly to digital queries.

3.6 Overseas student learning life adaptive challenge

Managing student experience in university life
challenge

What factors can influence international student's decision to choose where is abroad study destination . It links to the issue of how universities use knowledge to re-design machine and recruitment strategies towards international students. Commonly, there have three groups of factors that influence international students' decision on study destination which include communication, location and social factors. The sub-categories of these factors include quality of communications, study destination's attractiveness and social network. It is important to any universities need to understand the motivations and reasons international students choose certain programs/courses at a specific university. However, communication factors which has an important influence on international students' decision of study destination. The factors that encourage students to study abroad by examining push and pull factors. The push factors are defined as the factors that operate within the home country and initiate a student's decision to undertake international study when pull factors refer to dimensions within a study destination that make it attractive to international students.

On university communication to international student hand, nowadays, the digital age changes customers' views of convenience, speed, information and service (Armstrong, G, & Kotler, 2007). In fact, student's individual decision also study the existing activities carried out by the university of with regards to marketing and communication for prospective international applicants. The different communication channels to communicate with prospective students by the central unit technology include, such as when participating in education exhibitions and fairs. For example, participation in education exhibitions and fairs internationally in China, India and UK as well as locally is important. Some university department departments join local education exhibitions and fairs. The main purpose is to collect contracts and establish relationships with prospective students. When they return to themselves country, they can then provide further information and answer new queries with follow up email communication. The central unit technology highlights the relevance of parental influence and in certain cultures by targeting parents when who visit education exhibitions and fairs in India and China.

Furthermore, universities need to create a good first impression and build relationship with students, the central unit technology responds promptly to student queries. They understand that a quick and information response is important in separations themselves from their competitors. Prospective students cruise around different websites for information because they want to build relationships with prospective universities and right send email inquiries to several different universities. The university central online unit can join a forum, it is a forum when students/users can post provide assistance to users who have inquiries. For example, university central online unit can start an international ambassador organization. To help with student recruitment during education exhibitions and fairs. Also the university central online unit can maintain a face book page for graduated students. It can serve as an interaction platform for graduated current and prospective students with the university. Such as the central online unit can reach target students from India, China and Europe. They can run a social media challenge on face book that can also reach target UK and Chinese students. So, the university can serve as a pool of information of both current and prospective students. They emphasize that the website is always ranked high among students as a source of information. It is an important channel that provides information which is easily assessment. The following list is the online communication channels used by the different department in university. Such as, email channel is used to answer prospective students' inquiries. Online with universities communication and firms cooperation are introduced to let current students' experiences via recorded video, google advertisements are used to display the university and/or the department as the top option when users search online newsletters and online educational portals are used to connect interested students within specific fields with newsletters via cooperation with online education portals, photo blog. The publish current students' study experiences in the department with photos via blogs. Social media e.g. face book platform is used to provide an interactive platform with students, in special prospective students.

The final one is university website, it is used as the main communication channel link to different departments' own website and provide information. For example, local education exhibitions and fairs can join the central online unit to have face-to-face communication with prospective students, current student network exchange programs and to understand the current international students better, such as via annual brainstorming sessions. Also, lecturers and researcher's online network can promote the university through lecturer exchange and conferences abroad. Industrial network can maintain close relationships with the industries to create chances for students' career prospect.

How can communication channels and marketing communication influence students' decision making on study destination? It focuses on specifying the factors that influence international students' choices to study university destinations. Globalization and internationalization include recruitment of international students, staff exchanges between universities word wide. As globalization, it reflects global competitiveness process. This concept can be applied to consumer behavior theory to education by suggesting that students and their parents go through a few stages and eventually select an institution or subject of study. These stages include, such as pre-search behavior, search behavior, application , choice decision and registration stages. The first stage is pre-search behavior when students are in their early thoughts about their future. Next stage is search behavior stage, in this stage, students will gather information to get the shortlist of the potential study destination, institutions and courses. Then, it is the application stage, who will submit their applications to select institutions in the application stage. Next, it is choice destination occurs when students accept an offer, depending on the number of offers received. Finally, it is the register stage, during the register with the course. It seems the demand for study abroad and competitions in university sector makes international students' preferences an interesting subject to study. Thus, it is important for education marketers to know what factors that influence the purchase with university course choice intention of prospective students .

International student abroad study challenge
In general, students will follow these models to choose course. The first is economic models of student choice, which emphasize the costs aspects in relation to their studies, including the costs of choosing to study instead of work. The second is sociological models of student choice cover issues, such as family influences, personal motivation and ability and other influences. Finally, it is the information processing models of student choice combine both the economic and sociological models to determine the decision making of further study and the selection process of institutions. So, students decide to study abroad which is influences by push and pull factors at different stages. In first stage, students decide to study abroad with the influence of the push factors within the home country. In second stage, involves the selection of the study destination and students evaluate the factors which make one more attractive with pull factors. Lastly, students will select that institutions on third stage and these is additional pull factors make one institutions more attractive than its competitors, such as reputation, school fees, range of courses offered and staff expertise.

Summary, what factors influence students abroad study. There are variety of factors, such as access to local, perception of better quality of overseas teaching system, the availability of technology-based programs, the commonality of language and opportunity to improve second language, the geographic proximity of country, the institution's reputation for quality, the range of available programs/

courses and marketing efforts. So, an university's value is based on its relationship building and service delivery towards international students rather than on its facilities and student revenue. The main purpose influences students to further study abroad, especially to achieve personnel satisfaction further career. Commonly, students are buying the benefits that a degree can provide in favor of employment, status and lifestyles. However, influences and recommendations from family members, relatives, friends and professors also play an important role in a student's decision making process to study abroad. For example, Asian and African student are strongly influenced by their family. How universities should influenced by their families? How universities should market themselves to students? For example, Chinese students desire to improve their foreign language skills, are prefer to choose abroad as the study destination. The reasons are that the foreign degrees, e.g. UK are seen to have greater career value than Chinese degrees and that the experiences of living and working. How can attract more international students groups? To achieve this, communication play a crucial role. Communication occurs when a message is sent from a sender to a recipient with a purpose, an expression and a medium in a environment. Internet marketers customize and culture is a collective of interpretations that affects peoples' behaviors. It includes beliefs, values, social practice. They also highlight the link between culture and communication. When communication occurs across the internet, cultural aspects have to be across into account. The reason is the internet offers alternative communication channels like print media, word-of-mouth and public relations. Further, the internet allows markers to customize information that targets different cultures, including both verbal and non verbal content. Then, also highlight the importance of email communication of different languages on the website increases the attraction to receivers. So, it seems internet communication will be an advertisement strategy to assist any university to promote.

According to higher education survey, nearly half of all higher education institutes have experienced enrollment declines and consequently, shortfalls in net tuition revenue goals. Also many colleges need to take roughly 25 to 50% more staff time and effort to give students the levels of client service who expect. There is also no longer a single traditional educational degree. Institutions must accommodate the needs and preferences of students ranging from recent high school graduates to working adult learners. To meet enrollment and budget targets, institutions often attempt to introduce new multiple or double degree programs or to launch broad, institution wide advertising and marketing campaigns. However, it is like reasonable approaches, but results are often varied and unpredictable for two reasons: Such as, when extensive educational market research would give institutions a full understanding of their market opportunities and ideal targets, face have the internet resources necessary to carry it out. Another reason is without data to support their decisions, many institutions implement campaigns that don't differentiate the institution or its programs in ways that reason with today's students.

The key to enrollment growth and competitive strengths in today's higher education market is to offer the right programs to the right students. Using marketing and recruitment strategies in decision making will help boost enrollment, leading to more positive outcomes for both students and institutions. How to identify opportunities for improvements to existing programs that will help attract desired applicants and achieve targeted outcomes ? How to determine a degree program to institution's brand identity? Does a new program suit the institutions brand? Is the program consistent with the institution's loyalty and reputation?

The first suggestion is that researching employer demand for job market. Today, students concern on employment prospects. Corporations that have partnered with an institution can offer valuable insight into their priorities and perspectives on current and upcoming workforce requirements to help the college or university design new programs. Additionally, if particular geographic regions have traditionally provided high volumes of desirable applicants. The institution would gather input from employers to those more markets, then use that information to further refine degree programs to include practical, marketable skills and expertise. For example, incorporating specialties, such as concentrations, certification preparation, or study can help a degree program to develop. Then, collected data might also indicate areas where high schools industries or economic conditions are creating the most likely applicants. So, audience segmentation can include factors, such as political , per capita income, graduate vs undergraduate degrees, media usage and preferences etc.

My another suggestion is concerned these differentiate content for college target audiences, it has two sample categories both, such as first category is career climbers, headline can indicate to how to change course to achieve student individual dreams and to predict where endless opportunities are within reach. So, message can let audiences to feel real life experience and have flexible learning and career connections when who choose to study the university. Second, category is inactive military, headline can indicate to discover new ways to serve and where honor and integrity need precision and performance. So, message can let students to feel to get skills, discipline and experience and the university can have flexible learning options and tuition reimbursement for military service. There are sample communication messaging aligns both with each category and with the institution's existing brand and legacy. How institutions can make smart media choices to students? From owned to earn purchased to traditional, media outlets vary. When a broad mix gives greater exposure, choices should take each person's media preferences and psychological into account. This ensures that each selected channel is appropriate for reaching the target audiences. Also, prospective students can build ongoing relationships with advisors, which increases their engagement as well as institutions can make ongoing improvements by reviewing calls and gaining insight into problems and challenges prospective students may face. The most importance, it is a university can maintain complete records of all contacts. Because accurate, up-to-date records of communication frequency, response rates conversation histories, and schedules follow-up activities can help to ensure timeliness and to the marketing plan.

University life relationship to student challenge
In fact, college planning and management magazine estimates that institutions with " complete customer profiles with accurate data can increase revenue by 66%". So, customer relationship plan can help the university to accomplish to attract university students to enroll to choose to study of this task. Because customer relationship management plan can track such information allowing the recruiting process to run efficiently and making it easier to measure and refine activities that are tied to specific marketing and recruiting tactics. To optimize success, institutions must use research and planning to identify and target student's goals, then follow through with strong, personalized recruitment and enrollment efforts. Some institutions may choose to implement a complete marketing ad recruiting method to most efficiently and effectively make use of valuable resources to a complete marketing and recuritint service plan can help institutions build comprehensive, automized educational market research and recuriting initiative. The result: degree programs optimized for that institution's expertise and reputation and lead generation and recruitment strategies that target the institution's most promising applicants. The practices outlined can make dramatic differences in application volume ans yields when enabling marketing and recruiting efforts to operate more cost effectively and efficiently.

I shall indicate Malaysia educational system for public and private university attractive degree compare to explain why customer (student) relationship management plan is important. Malaysia includes public and private both institutions and it has public and private university, polytechnic, college, non-university status institutions and local or forcing university's branch campus. However, public universities in Malaysiz still attract the majority of undergraduate. Because public universities degree specification are recognized by the public services department, thus, individuals who hold degrees from public universities can work in the public sector, public universities are heavily subsidized by the government are therefore, fees are much cheaper than at private universities. Moreover, public universities can offer more places for professional and critical courses, e.g. medicine, dentistry, pharmaceutical studies, architecture, engineering, law, accounting with qualifications that are mostly and recognized by the respective local professional bodies and public universities provide students with a wider choice of programs in various fields of study.

Student applications for entry into bachelor's degree programs centralized processing agency. The agency of the ministry of higher division of student admission. Applicants need to provide a list of their choice of universities and programs and receive an offer from only one public university. In some case, the offer may even be from a university or program that was not included in the applicant's list of choices. However, the decision students make regarding their education revolves around several issues: first, students who finish their high school education must decide whether to pursue their tertiary education. Second, students who choose to further their education must take a choice regarding their program or field of education and institution of higher education and the institution of higher education.

Thus, in any university's customer relationship management plan, it can consist this first content, such as to find what factors can influence the students' choice of this specific institution of higher education. The tertiary institution choice modes include the following: economic models, sociological and combined models. Economic models of human capital investment emphasize rational decision ranking behavior when examining student's college choice. Students choose a college based on the level of value that each institution offers by comparing costs with perceived benefits. If the students feel the benefits of attending the institution are greater than the perceived benefits of enrolling in order institution.

The contribution of human capital investment factors, e.g. family income, tuition and financial aid on enrolments. For example, Ellwood and kane (2000) used a human capital income and college enrollment when controlling for academic ability, tuition and financial aid and preference (measured by parental education). Although the human capital investment model shows the effects of variables like income and ability on college related decision, it has limited usefulness in explaining source of difference in college choices across groups.

Next, in any university's customer relationship management plan, it can consist this second content, such as to find how to make the students choose this college to study. The combined models show a diversity of factors that influence students' choices. Some factors are related to the role of other persons, some are related to personal or individual factors and others are related to institutional characteristics and student perceptions about value and costs. Usually university causes negative relationship is caused by reputation of the institution, the program structure, the quality of the lecturers or families, the influence of the student's family and friends and customers (students) orientation in terms of entry (enrolling) requirement and availability of courses, courses fees, online or classroom teaching method, campus location etc. factors.

In general, the Asia country, Malaysia students concern these issues before who choose to study the university. The factors include: the demographic profile of the students, e.g. gender, age, ethnicity, the socio-economic background of the family, e.g. household income and parent education level and occupation, the reasons of the student pursue a higher education, the sources of information used in choosing a university college, and the factors that influence students' choice between public and private tertiary institutions etc. factors. All those factors will influence the Malaysia student who decides to choose to study the public or private tertiary institution finally. So, in their choosing procedure, Malaysia students will consider that factors are the importance of the various reasons for furthering whose education and then to specify which of the reasons is the most important.

Commonly Malaysia students who will consider whether the university will help them to find a good job, increase knowledge and to gain experience. Other reasons include fulfilment of parental expectations, interest in the field of study, enjoyment of campus life and the influence of their friends. In fact, Malaysis students can choose either of a public or private university to study. The factors influence them to choose include: the quality of education, lower tuition fee and access to financial assistance. However, the financial factors, e.g. lower tuition fee of education and available financial assistance in public institutions are extremely important considerations to influence their choice. Other factor is the quality of education provided by the public or private university. The key performance indicators (kpds) report indicated that students in public universities are assured of receiving high quality tertiary education because the efficiency and productivity of public universities, that encompass various aspects, such as teaching and learning, employability of students and social responsibility (Universiti, Teknologi MARA, 2009).

In general, for science students, who will concern about whether the university can provide enough facilities to have been made available to them to carry on researching in campus environment, which include the following: teaching facilities, computer and research laboratories, lecture hall, complex equipped with state of the art multimedia systems etc. excellent library facilities, sports facilities and other supporting facilities, such as a book store, a health center and book services.

Finally, I suggest university information ought to be highlighted in university's website because the internet and university websites are the source of information must frequently used by students to make their choice of tertiary education institution. Because students consider the availability of a course or program that who wish to pursue as another extremely important consideration to study in Malaysia public or private university. However, it is necessary to keep abreast with changes in the higher education and the contemporary demands from the working world require review of program and courses. To design new courses that balance the diverse needs of students and the emerging needs of the educational and labor markets in Malaysia. For example, the school of social sciences in Malaysia university, which is the focus of this study is planning in the near future to introduce two new program. Bachelor of social work program and a bachelor of Economics program. The two new courses will include various courses in new areas of study that are emerging in these disciplines.

To conclude, new to focus on various factors in order to attract students of high quality to its undergraduate courses, the university will be able to nurture students for post graduate studies higher education program as a research university. Such as in Malaysia rapidly growing education sector, it must transform itself into a world class university, so that it can attract the best students and produce the best graduates in the country.

Finally, in the university's client relationship management plan, it needs to find what the variety of trends to develop recruitment and technology and enrollment and branding within higher education marketing is for the university. Nowadays, the variety of trends to higher education marketing. Such as many universities have hires marketing professionals from the corporate world, who have invested significant time and money to create strong institutional brands. The online and digital space is using technology to its full potential, particularly with social media and other platforms, for graduates recruitment service in universities. Also, recruitment strategies in higher education increasingly focus on international students and non-traditional and adult learners.

Online of continuing education program will be popular to be taught to online students. Adaptive learning technology has also enjoyed significant interest to let students feel new learning method. Successful branding and marketing have become increasingly important activities for institutions. Every university needs to differentiate itself from computer institutions. Successful branding can help with increasing enrollment, expanding fundraising capabilities, and other outcomes.

How to communicate a brand to build confidence and famous university image to students? However, there is evidence that universities don't have to spend significant amounts of money to promote online advertisement to be effective. For example, institutions need image have more emphasis on responsive web design to create university online advertisement and easy to navigate websites that can viewed on multiple devices and platforms. Also administrators want their universities to receive a prominent spot in search engine results particularly googles. Especially for institutions that offer niche courses. It is increasingly important to ensure that research results include these courses at the top rank. Also, colleges and universities can rely on data driven analytics to determine who, how and where who are reaching their audiences. The use of analytics software is increasing as the higher education web ecosystem is becoming expanding (domains, subdomains etc.) Getting a better handle of this data is a new area of concentration for colleges and universities.

Some form of social media, e.g. face book or twitter accounts will be popular to accept to attract to see university's online advertisement. Also the rise of mobile technology and connected devices, colleagues and universities are making greater investments in having a mobile presence. This includes not only mobile versions of university websites and other content. Beyond, the changes are brought by teaching, marketing and branding trends have shown more creatively outreach efforts, as well as design and advertising campaigns. However, more traditional marketing and branding strategies, such as open house events and sponsored visits for students are also extremely popular.

I feel any university needs to build its brand to let different country's students know. Branding requires patient and effort and relies heavily on timing. A university brand can be damaged much more quickly than it can be successfully built. So, consistency purpose and messaging is necessary. For instance, a series of low university rankings can do long term damage to the image. It is very important to keep promises, particularly when it comes to the quality of the education provided. Institutions must be committed to maintaining and improving quality. Universities' communications must constantly be facts, data and evidence: rankings, applicant data (number and quality), recruitment of professors, placement of graduates, media presence, that demonstrates the quality, as the excellence of the institutions helps and strengthens its brand for long term.

One of the most significant ways branding and marketing of higher education has changed in recent years has been in the online space, using a variety of new platforms for external social and digital platforms. To achieve this, it ahs become common for universities to ensure home page is clearly laid out portal to all of the content that students are looking for online. This means websites often have new feature elements, such as well placed navigation bars and engaging visuals, e.g. slideshow, multimedia, content etc. So, broader tends in the use of social media platforms, however, have shown that when their use of colleges, universities, community colleges and other academic institutions. Also, there are a number of tends in recruitment and enrollment that are having a significant impact on how institutions go about attracting. There are a number of trends in recruitment and enrollment students knowing consumers' education tuition what level is reasonable issue is important factor, that are having a significant impact on how institutions go about attracting students. It includes demographics and increased mobility of students, as well as the increasing cost of higher education in many countries.

Firstly, I shall indicate the recent higher education trends for enrollment and recruitment references hand. Such as: education cost trend, effect or impact to many families concern experiencing a diminished ability to pay for a college education compared to pre-recession levels, median household income, home equity and net worth are all down. Meanwhile, commonly global college tuition costs have continued to climb steadily, even after financial aid is factored in. Even more families are re-evaluating the education tuition, who are willing to pay for a college education. Commonly, the cost of a college education is climb up against the ceiling of what education. The cost of a college education is climbing up against the ceiling of what families will consider paying. Even, students from upper-middle income families are experiencing higher levels of student debt and factoring in the cost of post-graduate study of majoring in certain fields. So what major subject choice at the course factor will influence the student feel whether the tuition is reasonable or unreasonable to pay. Even, media coverage and legislative attention are shaping public opinion about the value of a college education is necessary a value gap which has opened up in the polling because far fewer people believe going to college at any price will be worth the financial investment. It seems some public universities which get government funders' assistance can make their appropriations contingent upon institutional better performance measures. In fact, families are seeking evidence of successful results to justify their college investment. Higher education has become less and end itself and increasingly a means to an end primarily an economically viable career factor in outcomes as well as cost. Students will expect proof of high graduation rates and graduate employment at acceptable salary levels.

Secondly, on different demographics trend hand, the number of high school graduates is shrinking, but the proportion that is ethically diverse is growing. The country's changing demographics, combined with a widening gap between the nation's rich and poor, mean more first generation students and students from socio-economic background that not only make paying for college a challenge, but also often leave them underprepared for college level study.

Thirdly, In the study aging trend hand, non-traditional age students still represent a largely expanding market. During the economic recession, more people age 25 and older returned to college, but that reached its peak in 2020 year prior record. But nontraditional students also more likely to leave out in their first year. So who seek convenient course scheduling, assistance is the financial aid process, tutoring ad counseling services.

Fourthly, on the transfers of university hand, more students are attending multiple institutions in their pursuit of a degree. Transferring is increasingly becoming a cost-conscious part of students' long term plans to affordable degree completion. In general, students who transfer from a private non profit institution attend two year public institutions, with four year public institutions being their second most popular destination. On university student of consumption behavior engaged consumers hand, growth in mobile online access and social media use is allowing people to instantly verify any claims a college makes.

Generation connected is not bound by age brackets, but rather by shared behavior, this is used of real time social, local and mobile technology. They find it increasingly easy to investigate institution's reputations via online networks, word-of-mouth recommendations and other communication channels beyond the colleges' direct control. Students like to investigate any universities' target data from internet channels.

The widespread use of data analytics in other industries is leading students to expect personalized and relevant communications. The digital information that can be captured about even those students who don't explicitly make their interest known to be college has enhanced targeting capabilities. And since private non profit institutions are known for providing personal attention, families do note any disconnects in that any university brand attribute during the admissions process.

Finally, on the online education trend, the proliferation of massive open online courses is drawing attention to how college credits are awarded. All types of online and hybrid courses are be popular to university marketplace seeks cost effective access and convenient delivery. So the university student segment will be popular to online courses teaching channel to any international college in the future.

Also, advertising is important promotion method to let students know that the university is update message. Among the least effective strategies and tactics for both private and public four year institutions were radio advertising, the popular advertising will be online college fairs and billboard/ bus/outdoor advertising. However, running television advertisement was rested a top practice, it is possible that television advertising can give visual enjoyment to attract student audience attention. Also the preferred method of communication with potential students, it will be sending email , however, though mailers and brochures are still used by a significant number of institutions.

The international university education competition, among the most competitive areas of colleges and universities increasingly across the globe is the international/foreign student market. The U.S., Britain, Australia and other English speaking countries are competing for largely the same students and some warn that the number of courses available to international students in these countries will outstrip the number of students on the education market. So, the combination of increased mobility of students and the lower number of first time applicants at universities in English speaking countries has created pressures to compete for international students. In addition, any country also needs have good marketing and recruitment strategy for graduate students. It aims to attract international students. For example, some institutions have elected to hire companies, such as the Pearson employment firm's progression and "website gives students most likely exam clients admission and " pathway information on universities that partner with Pearson.

The U.S. has been particularly success in its recruitment of international students, particularly Chinese students. To achieve Chinese student to choose U.S. institutions have had to change their strategies for recruitment, such as maintaining a presence at conferences and job fairs overseas offering generous financial aid packages to international students as well as improving social media outreach effort. Some university students who are adult learners. Outside of international student recruitment trends in higher education indicate that another key audience for enrollment is adult and non traditional learners.

In the United States, the number of adult learners returning to higher education. So, the student individual age will be increased to 25 age and over and this pattern is expected to continues. The reason is possible that some adult students who are working and who feel whose employers need them to raise knowledge to achieve the educational acceptance level to feel who has effort to do the job. It will predict that the percentage of enrollments for students 25 age and older will increase by 20% over 2010 year. So, it will be global education trend, the adult student target segment will increase in global education market. However, recruiting those adult students will encounter an unmet demand and growing market segment for both countries and who required recruitment strategies that speak directly to this demographic. When some of the employment methods are the same as recruiting traditional students , e.g. quality, communication methods, effective websites, using social media etc. other trends are noticeable in how institutions make their programs more attractive to adult learners. zone of the most common course design to highly flexible programs that can meet the needs of working adult learners, including expanding offering in the part and evening course different adult student segment needs and to satisfy the number of options for online education. Additional improving lead educational quality when identifying adult students and designing adult learn programs specifically adult students as opposed to adopt existing programs.

In summary, University (education) industry examines the effects of lowered admissions standards on universities facing both lower graduation rates and reductions in state funding. For university rank, international student, in special Asian or non english nature language students, who choose overseas universities to enroll, who will concern the institutions. So universities can provide to relax standards in other areas to boost their international enrollments in particular, such as required language proficiency, in favor of admitting those students that exhibit strong academic backgrounds. A trend in recent years for U.S. institutions has been to admit international students with weak language skills about strong academic skills on a conditional basis, allowing students to strengthen language abilities once admitted. These types of admissions are often called " intensive English enrollments" and several institutions have reported a distinct increase in enrollments as a result of such admissions policies that feature language programs. Hence, if the university required high level English language proficiency ability to enroll to study any courses, then it will attract more potential English language students to enroll in this global competition education market. Otherwise, the lower English language level institutions will encounter to loss more. Besides, the classroom which typical lecture and homework of a a course are reversed and in classroom experiences reconstructed to rely less on passive learning and more an active engagement. Because university students concern how to consume the core elements of a course whenever, regardless of time or place. This mean professors can re-allot classroom time completely and make a room for other activities, such as experimental or collaborative learning opportunities as opposed to passive learning through lecturers.

Thus, it seems how university can attract more students to study, it depends on lecturer's individual teaching method or choosing what kind of education courses to be taught to whose students. It will influence students have good or bad emotion or feeling to learn. So, university needs to concern lecturer's teaching methods to let students to feel satisfactory. Also, where the university campus location choice is another factor to influence student choice as well as student learning experience to the university etc. factors will be the most influential to any students to choose which university to study finally. So, educators need to concern these issues.

3.7 Internet influences E-education service teaching performance

Nowadays, many businesses are international trading, due to globalization and opening of markets. E-commerce will be the most popular
advertisement and sale method to help any kinds of businesses to promote products to let many clients to know effectively in short time. However, e-ecommerce will bring new organizational structure change to help any organizations to improve performance management, organizational development, and continuous and cumulative process of improvement of multi-national companies, when the organization can have e-commerce sale strategy. I believe that one effective e-commerce strategy can influence any educational service organizations to raise their educational learning level. I shall explain the reasons as below:

On innovation and e-educational teaching and learning platform for raising the school's teaching attractive level aspect, it can bring rapid students increase , many graduates and improving its teaching method advantage to let its online students to feel, it also needs the teaching leader or school leader has clear online teaching vision to create and maintain his school learning organization, such as the e-learning and teaching platform, e.g. how to improve itself school's learning and teaching platform to be more attractive and has more influential to be one successful e-teaching and learning organization. When the school decides to provide online platform to let students to learn, it is a e-educational middleman to help students can stay in their homes to learn distance education conveniently. When any distance learning students can click the school website to choose any courses to learn and they can follow the school's time table to learn from the online classroom environment, they can enquire the teacher to let they can know the answer to solve the learning problem from the teacher's e-learning platform immediately. So, if the school e-learning platform can provide rapid e-learning delivery service to let them to feel e-learning service satisfactory feeling. Hence, if the school can provide continuous e-learning method in its leadning organizational life, a rapid and efficient and attrative e-learning process can help every online or distance learning student how he/she feels himself /herself e-learning understanding satisfactory feeling, self-e-learning management and himself/herself e-learning e-learning actualization of feeling . However, the successful factors of e-learning platform are needed to concern on how to raise the e-learning organization's e-platform innovation and delivery an efficient and attractive e-learning teaching service, providing skillful online e-education and online learning management skills are its main successful factors. Moreover, any e-learning organizatins can apply psychological knowledge to assist any one e-learning student to feel this e-learning platform can raise e-learning effort to let them to understand any courses in the more efficiency to compare the traditional classroom learning method.

In fact, e-learning technique innovation will be another factor to raise any e-learning organization competitive effort, e.g. reducing distance learning students need to spend long time to learn any new knowledge from online classroom. So, when the e-learning organization can raise new e-learning technique to help its distance learning students to spend much learning time to compare traditional classroom learning method. Then, it will let its distance learning students to feel reducing finance burden and learning time burden to learn the e-learning organization's online courses for long time. Hence, an successful e-learning can provide low cost e-learning service technique and less learing time , but they can learn any new knowledge from the online teachers absolutely.

IN one successful e-learning educational environment, since internet is popular, it can influence the school's distance learning students feel its online learning is better than traditional classroom. So,if the e-learning organization can provide, such as rapid e-library book borrow service and e-reading method and rapid e-book seek information search in safe and quiet home learning environment, even public library environment or anywher and any time. It can still let them to feel none any e-learning difficulties, due to the e-learning organization's poor learning time arrangement and poor learning enquiry arrangement. They can still feel learning satisfaction , then the e-learning organization ought attract many distance learning students choose it to study to compare other e-learning schools.

Bibliography

Armstrong & Kotler, P.(2007).Marketing on introduction (8th ed.), Upper Saddle River, New Jersey: Person Education, Inc.

Dickinson, K.D. Pollock, A, & Troy, J. (1995), " perceptions of the value of quality assessment in scottis higher education", Assessment and evaluation in higher education, vol. 20, no 1, pp. 59-66.

Ellwood, D.T. and T.J. kane (2000). Who is getting a college education? Family background and growing gaps in enrollment. In securing the future investing in children from birth to college, eds. S. Daneiger and J. Waldfoges 283-324. New York: Russe Sage Foundation.

Eshach, H. (2009). The Nobel Prize In The Physics Class: Science, history and glamour. Science & Education, 18, 1377-1393. doi: 10.1007/s
11191-008-9172-4.

Ferguson, Y., & Sheldon, K.M. (2010). Should goal
strivers, think about "why " or "how" to strive?
It depends on their skill level. Motivation and
emotion 34-253-265.

Fosnot, C. (1989). Enquiring teachers, enquiring learners. New York: Teachers college press.

Harvey, L. & Green, D. (1993) " Defining quality",
Assessment and evaluation in higher education,
vol, 18, pp.8-35.

Horn, H.L. & Murphy, M.D. (1985). Low need achievers' performance: The positive impact of
a self-determined goal. Personality and social
psychology Bulletin, 11, 275-285.

Huang, H.I. (2012). An empirical analysis of the strategic Management of competitive advantage: a case study of higher technical and vocational education in Taiwan (Doctoral dissertation, Victoria University).

Kim, Y. J., and J.W. Lee 2009. Technological Change, Human Capital Structure and Multiple Growth Paths, ADB Economics Working Paper Series No. 149, Economics And Research Dept. Asian Development Bank, Manila.

Kim, Y. J., and J.W. Lee 2009. Technological Change, Human Capital Structure and Multiple Growth Paths, ADB Economics Working Paper Series No. 149, Economics And Research Dept. Asian Development Bank, Manila.

Marzano, R.J., Pickering, D.J., & Pollock, J.E. (2001). Classroom instruction that works. Alexandria, VA: ASCD.

Qualters, D. (2001). Do students want to be active? The Journal of job.

Schunk, D.H., & Rice, J.M. (1991). Learning goals and progress feedback instruction. Journal of reading behavior. 23, 351-364.

Trigwell, K., Prosser, M. & Waterhouse, F. (1999) Relations Between Teachers' Approaches To Teaching And Students' Approaches To LearningHigher Education 37: 57-70.

Universiti teknologi, MARA 2009, Key performance indicators (kpis, for governance of public universities in Malaysia, Shah Alam: Asian Centre for Research On University Learning and Teaching) ACRULET. Universiti, teknologi MARA.